D1611792

LIKE NO OTHER CAREER

by

MARVIN TRAUB
former chairman of Bloomingdale's

AND LISA MARSH

For Lee, who continues to make life more wonderful.

© 2008 Assouline Publishing
601 West 26th Street, 18th Floor
New York, NY 10001, USA
www.assouline.com

ISBN: 978 2 75940 272 4

Printed in China

All rights reserved. No part of this publication may be
reproduced or transmitted in any form or by any means,
electronic, or otherwise, without prior consent of the publisher.

LIKE
NO OTHER CAREER

by

MARVIN TRAUB
former chairman of Bloomingdale's

AND LISA MARSH

ASSOULINE

Lee and Marvin meeting
Marvin, I must say you did a great job for
Karl Lagerfeld oct '91

CONTENTS

Karl Lagerfeld's wonderful concept of Lee and me meeting Coco Chanel. We always had a very close relationship with Karl, whether it was backstage after a show or a luncheon at his château in Paris after he lost 91 pounds.

big
brown
bag

FOREWORD

BY SUE KRONICK, *vice-chair, Macy's, Inc.*

Nobody knew for sure what Chairman Marvin Traub was going to do after he left Bloomingdale's, in 1991—but his process of leaving was as carefully orchestrated as the theatrical international promotions and events he brought to the American retail scene twenty years earlier. There were European designer farewells in Paris; individual store tours with emotional poetry readings from sales associates; buried time capsules; and a fully costumed marching band, horns a-blazing, traveling down "B'way" past thousands of employees and a slightly misty-eyed Marvin. He would have had it no other way.

Many of us who had the privilege of working with Marvin for several decades learned firsthand the power that passion, leadership, and vision can deliver. In the beginning, there was no printed mission statement, but everybody—even the executive trainees—knew the goal: to bring unique and exclusive merchandise, as well as theater, art, education, and celebrity pizzazz, to the shopping experience.

Marvin is a matchmaker who has a nose for talent. Early on, he identified promising European and American designers and developed partnerships with them to build their brands. This seems academic today, but he was always looking for the next

The Bloomingdale's Big Brown Bag, created twenty-five years ago by Massimo and Lela Vignelli, and still in use.

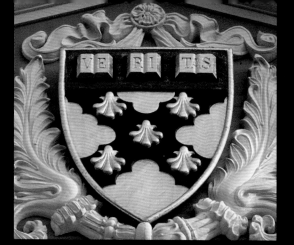

unique risk to take or the next person to believe in. He respected talented people, even if they had difficult or impossible personalities, because he understood that brilliance is rare—and when he found it, he nurtured it. This was true both inside and outside of Bloomingdale's. At last count, there are more than forty people with whom he has worked closely or has personally developed who became or are principals today. Marvin's eye for young designer and retail talent, along with his thoughtfulness about their business and career growth, is clearly one of his most lasting gifts to our industry.

It's not really a surprise that Marvin's post-Bloomingdale's career has been so packed with energy and change. He remains voraciously curious about ideas and people, and so his average two-breakfasts, two-dinners, flight-to-somewhere day hasn't changed much over the years. Just as he has always actively promoted his current ventures, he remains fascinated by new people and opportunities. He's a connector. He works at it, and it keeps him young.

On a more personal level, Marvin has known me since I was born, as he and my father, Albert Kronick, were Harvard Business School classmates. It may be fair to say that with the exception of my parents, Marvin has been one of my most important mentors, but then there is a very long list of people, whether by osmosis or directly, who could make the same claim. However, in the end, what has proven true again and again is that one person can make a difference to individuals and to an entire industry. Marvin has done just that.

(*Top*) The Harvard Business School crest. (*left, right*) Sue Kronick and I at two of our industry black-tie dinners. In 2007, I cochaired the 59th Parsons Benefit and Fashion Show honoring Sue, where Bill Clinton and Oscar de la Renta spoke. (*bottom*) Me smoking a pipe in my office in the 1960s.

nom de Jacques Mouclier, Pierre Bergé et
moi même. Au nom de tous nos amis -
nom de la France entière. Au nom de la
e en France, du Luxe, de la Beauté, de la
, du savoir vivre en France. Nous
mes heureux et fiers de vous re mettre ce
u .

haque page nous avons mis une part d
e coeur . A chaque page nous vous redison
e admiration pour votre grande et magnifi
lité (si rare dans notre metier) pour votre feul
e votre capacité folle de travail, votre
ence. Vous êtes un homme tr pressé et
avez toujours le temps d'écouter . Merci
et Martin, Paris ne sera jamais pare
s vous . On vous attend et on vou
ne .

Sonia R Mul

INTRODUCTION

This book began on a beautiful day in the summer of 2006 in one of my favorite cities, Paris. That afternoon, a charming couple, Prosper and Martine Assouline, joined Lee and me for lunch in the gardens of the Hôtel Ritz. I had gotten to know Prosper when one of his associates approached me about writing a book. I wasn't sure if the offer was serious, so the four of us had a delightful lunch—the only kind one has at the Ritz in Paris.

Prosper said it would be a marvelous idea to bring readers up to date on recent activities in my career and on my beliefs about retailing. The more I drank the Puligny-Montrachet and ate our Salad Gourmande, the better the proposal sounded. I thought there were three goals to be accomplished in such a book: It would be an opportunity to publish some wonderful sketches presented to Lee and me by leading European designers at our farewell party; to share some observations about what is happening in the retail industry today; and most important, to discuss my second career, because I feel

(Opposite) This is a translation of the first page of the folio by Sonia Rykiel: *On behalf of Jacques Mouclier, Pierre Bergé and myself, on behalf of all your friends and all of France. In the name of France, of luxury, of beauty, and on behalf of French "joie de vivre," we are happy and proud to submit this book. On each page, we put a piece of our hearts. On each page, we tell you over and over again our admiration for your great and magnificent personality, for your kindness and your amazing capability to work, and for your presence and easy manner. You are a man in a hurry, but you always have time to listen. So, thank you—Paris will never be the same without you. We always await your return and we love you. Sonia Rykiel.*

passionately that businessmen and women should be able to go forward after their primary careers have ended to find success and fulfillment in new ventures. I was fortunate to have written a book about my life and career through 1993, *Like No Other Store: The Bloomingdale's Legend and the Revolution in American Marketing*, and to write a second volume detailing my activities through the present seemed like a wonderful idea.

As I look back, I have had an extraordinary and fulfilling series of careers from my start at Bloomingdale's, in 1950, through the beginning of my second career, in 1992.

Some twenty-four members of the staff of our Bloomingdale's buying office in Paris, AMC, lined up for a farewell photo on the balcony of 14, rue de Castiglione. Between 1954 and 1991, I visited Paris more than a hundred times.

At the same time, I've witnessed the dramatic changes that occurred in American retailing: first, between the end of World War II and 1993, and then in the more recent era of consolidation and globalization. By the time our dessert menus came around, I was sold on the idea of writing a new book—one that would cover the many exciting aspects of my new career and provide an opportunity for me to express my belief that second careers can keep one young, committed, and involved in life.

EUROPEAN DESIGNERS AND FRIENDS WISH ME A FOND FAREWELL

In October 1991, I attended the Paris *prêt-à-porter*, or ready-to-wear, collections as chairman of Bloomingdale's. I was excited by the event, knowing that I was going to retire in just four weeks, on November 15th. In honor of my retirement, Chantal Rousseau, then Bloomingdale's vice president for Europe; Jean-Louis Dumas, the chairman of Hermès; and many designers gave a farewell party for me at the Hôtel Crillon, in Paris, on October 21.

Now that I was leaving Bloomingdale's, Chantal wanted to make sure that my departure was given the proper fanfare, and it was a great party. My friends Pierre Bergé, Didier Grumbach, president of the Fédération Française de la Couture; Jacques Mouclier, honorary president of the Chambre de la Haute Couture; fashion designer Sonia Rykiel; and Chantal presided over the festivities. They invited a host of European designers, manufacturers, and friends that I had made during my forty years at Bloomingdale's, most of which had included at least two or three visits to Paris.

The high point of the party was the presentation of an exquisite leather-bound folio, specially created by Hermès to house unique works of art, which each of the European designers had dedicated to my wife, Lee, and me with their thoughts about us.

"I wanted to surprise Marvin with something that nobody ever, ever, could give him," Chantal elaborates. "I wanted it to be really first, first class, because, you know, Marvin loves everything to be perfect. I asked Hermès to do the bookbinding and then I sent everybody a page with an explanation of what was expected. I said it was only for Marvin—nobody would read it before, so it could be very personal. Every page in these books is one-of-a-kind."

At the time of the Paris event, there was only one folio. But as other designers wanted to be included, we acquired enough original artwork to fill a second volume. All in all, there were seventy works of art included. Unfortunately, we could only choose a certain number to be reproduced in this book, but each of them brings back very special memories for me and for Lee.

Sous le haut patronage de
la Chambre Syndicale du Prêt à porter
des Couturiers et des Créateurs de mode,
Pierre Bergé, Sonia Rykiel, Jacques Mouclier
les Grands Magasins Bloomingdale's sont heureux de vous inviter
le lundi 21 octobre à L'hotel de Crillon
en l'honneur de
Marvin S. Traub,
Chairman of the Board
qui doit quitter ses fonctions le 15 novembre
et pour rencontrer
Michael Gould,
son successeur

✱

Cocktail
17h-19h 30
Hôtel de Crillon
Place de la Concorde

R.S.V.P. Chantal Rousseau
c/o AMC
14, rue de Castiglione - 75001 Paris
Tel: 42 60 34 03

1. Sonia Rykiel, Pierre Bergé, and Marvin Traub. 2. Marvin with Suzy Menkes. 3. Marvin and Lee with Count Rene de Chambrun. 4. Marvin and Carla Fendi. 5. Jean-Louis Dumas and Marvin. Dumas was then C.E.O. of Hermès and created the folio for the designer's artwork. 6. Christian Lacroix, Marvin, and Louis Vuitton's Henry Recamier. 7. Chantal Rousseau, Mike Gould, Lee, and Marvin. 8. Jean Taittinger and Marvin. Jean, then C.E.O. of the Taittinger group, owned the Crillon and other hotels, and Taittinger Champagne. 9. Carla Fendi, Marvin, and Claude Montana. 10. Marvin, Ines de la Fressange (in the background), Karl Lagerfeld, and Chantal Rousseau. 11. Jacques and Louise Rouet with Lee and Marvin. Jacques was then C.E.O. of Christian Dior.

7

8

9

10

11

Emanuel Ungaro is a designer whom Lee and I consider a close personal friend. He used to invite me to have a glass of champagne with him and preview his collection the day before he showed it. During the collections, Katie Murphy our fashion director; Dick Hauser, our general merchandise manager; Lee and I would eat dinner with him on Sunday evenings just after he showed his collection. He was not only talented but also was a warm, charming person who designed complex combinations of prints and styles. This drawing is reminiscent of his look. I believe he was inspired by Asians who came to France in the seventeenth century looking for French products. If you look closely, he put Bloomingdale's in the middle of the desert and me in an Arabian court.

(Collection Yves Saint Laurent Rive Gauche
Automne/Hiver 1991-92

Dear Marvuin,

   Votre chaleur, votre amitié, votre courtoisie et
votre ouverture m'ont permis de découvrir que
des discussions d'affaires permettaient aussi d'aimer
les personnes.

                              Avec toute mon affection

                              Maurice CAN

                              Yves Saint Laurent Rive Gauche

To MARVIN
WITH
Love
Yves Saint Laurent

(Opposite) Winter '92 collection. The letter is from Maurice Cau, managing director of YSL.

(This page) Yves always loved red hearts. We started with Yves Saint Laurent when he did his first collection for America. He was owned by our good friend Dick Salomon, who owned Lanvin-Charles of the Ritz. One of my favorite Saint Laurent stories took place in 1974 when he had a party at 21. Lee—that was before she became fluent in French—was speaking to him in French. "Let's speak English," Yves said. "My English is better than your French."

Bloo~~X~~ingdale's

sans Lea

et sans

Marvin

quelques

choses va

manquer à

Bloomingdale's

Ralph   love Kane

In the mid-sixties, Bloomingdale's buyers had been through the entire accessory sector looking for new names, but without success. Then Marvin Traub came to Rome to personally look for new brands. Walking down the via Borgognona, he was dazzled by our new line with the double f. He entered the boutique. I was there and he introduced himself and decided on the spot to dedicate a space to fendi at Bloomingdale's.

In the seventies, Marvin was the first one to encourage us to do a ready-to-wear line (he used to say that the clothes worn under the furs, made only for the shows, were beautiful, but too bad it was not possible sell them). And so the first RTW collection was born, contributing to the growth of fendi.

At the end of the eighties, Marvin Traub supported the launch of the first fendi fragrance. In one night he decided to change the whole scenery of the cosmetic department after we told him it did not correspond to our image. In this occasion Marvin taught us something very important that only great personalities know how to do, and that is to admit the proper faults and then make a change.

Carla fendi

(Opposite page) Great sketch, all five Fendi sisters at their shop greeting me—Paula, Alda, Franca, Carla, and Fe. The saga began in the 60s, when I was walking along the Via Condotti in Rome and saw an attractive shop that had luggage in the window. I went in and saw they had great looking handbags as well. "Do you sell in America?" I asked. "Oh yes," one of the shopgirls replied. "We sell our luggage." "Who do you sell it to?" "We sell it to Bendel's. They are our exclusive agent." "Bloomingdale's would be a wonderful opportunity," I suggested. I doubt if the shop girl knew what Bloomingdale's was. Then I asked for Carla Fendi, and it all began. We opened the first Fendi shop in America at the corner of 60th Street and became very friendly with the entire Fendi family—particularly Carla.

Thierry Mugler

To Marvin who's a great figure of the fashion world! Sincerely Thierry!

ierry Mugler, the French designer, is very interested in dance—he has that in common with Lee. We launched his llection by taking over Studio 54 in New York in the early 1970s for a great party and fashion show. I think he is a great nt. This unique picture was taken from the roof of the Palais Garnier, which houses the Opera National de Paris

En témoignage de nos rencontres passées
recevez ce dessin de vase unique.

M Lalique

le 21 Octobre 1991

Lalique had been a wonderful name in the late nineteenth century, and at that time it was a product for collectors and museums, not a business for department stores. Marie-Claude Lalique, the designer of the collection, succeeded her father Marc. Lalique was launched by her grandfather, Rene. Marie-Claude was a successful artist as well as a designer and inscribed the sketch "as a testimony of our past meetings" and for our role in helping Lalique move into other channels, meaning department stores.

TO MARVIN
        our „godfather"
with best wishes and love
rosita · ottavio Missoni
                oH. 91

28

We used to call him our "Godfather." Marvin, President and then Chairman of the "Swinging Bloomingdale's" in 1969, was the very first to trust our talent. We owe him our first appearances in a store, our first full-page advertisements in the *New York Times*, our first beautiful store windows and our first home collections in the early seventies with fieldcrest. Since then, we built a very close friendship and we never miss an opportunity to get together. We were touched when Marvin showed up to the party celebrating our fiftieth anniversary. God bless Marvin!

Ottavio and Rosita Missoni

(Opposite) When Tai and Rosita Missoni were just starting out, Leonard Rosenberg, our ready-to-wear vice president, discovered them in Milan. I thought what they were doing was unique and extraordinary. Bloomingdale's launched them in the states, their business grew, and we grew as personal friends as well. Our daughter Peggy vacationed with the Missonis and their children on an island just off Trieste. They shouted at her just the way they shouted at their own children, so we knew Peggy was family. They are great family people. Tai is an extraordinary textiles designer and Rosita a talented apparel designer, which makes for a unique collaboration. Tai actually competed as a long-distance runner in the 1952 Olympics.

(This page) Jean-Paul Gaultier is one of the true geniuses of our industry. He is warm, passionate and generous. I am very appreciative of his note commenting on my very early support of his house. He is one of a small number of European designers that were outstanding in the 1980s and are still outstanding today. He is unusual in that his own collection and that of Hermès, which he also designs, are so different, yet equally successful. I like the sketch he did of his head.

(Opposite) Great picture of Issey Miyake with his five different collection labels and a gracious note, "My history started with you." When we first visited Japan, Lee thought Issey was charming as well as a real genius, and so did I. We became good friends. The whole world regarded him as unique. Bloomingdale's launched him, but there was competition. Even though Issey and I were close, Bergdorf Goodman built a shop on its main floor to attract him. That's the apparel business!

issey miyake

issey miyake

issey miyake

issey miyake
PARIS · TOKYO · NEW YORK

SEY MIYAKE

Dear Lee
and Marvin
My history
started
with you.
Best Wishes

Oct. 1991

31

Dear Lee & Marvin,
we'll miss you!
A thousand thanks
& Love
from

Christian Lacroix and I have been good friends for many years. We share a love for his native Provence, the region that inspired his brilliant colors and prints that set him apart from other designers and made him a great success in couture.

DEAR MARVIN   DEAR LEE —

HU-BEAR WILL NEVER FORGET YOUR
FRIENSHIP AND YOUR HELP FOR MY "BLOOMI
SHOPPING"
    I DO RESPECT YOU VERY MUCH —
WITH ALL MY ADMIRATION FOR BOTH OF
YOU — WITH MY LOVE —

Hubert de Givenchy is a very good friend. When we launched the Givenchy fragrance, he brought Audrey Hepburn to Bloomingdale's, which drew a large, excited crowd. We created and presented to him the Hu-Bear, a cuddly teddy bear wearing a miniature version of the white coat that Givenchy wore to design in. He loved it and it became part of his permanent collection. So he drew Hu-Bear as a reminder to us. Hubert is a true aristocrat among designers. I enjoyed working with him, and Lee and I treasure his friendship.

This is a drawing of Lee and me by Sonia Rykiel. Sonia, before the days of the tents, used to do shows in her own showroom at 7 rue de la Grenelle and as her models would come down the spiral staircase, she would read poetry. It was an intellectual happening. There would be a good many people jammed into this tiny space including Gerry Stutz of Henri Bendel, Lee, me, and the Bloomingdeale's buyers. It was very intimate and special. When the tents arrived, the entire mood changed and it became much more commercial.

Cresson

I met Edith Cresson, France's prime minister at that time, when she was minister for trade. We worked together to increase French exports to the U.S., and I supported her when she sent a trade delegation to the states. We had a great mutual respect and friendship. Five years earlier, she was one of the people who recommended me for the Légion d'Honneur. She was known as the prime minister who wore Dior.

Franco Moschino had a marvelously irreverent sense of humor. In 1991, we were to receive $1 million in support from the Italian government for our upcoming Ecco Italia promotion. We persuaded Moschino to design our shopping bag. Tongue-in-cheek, he designed a bag that featured the Statue of Liberty with the saying "In Pizza We Trust" on one side, and a gorgeous model in a dress made from the Italian flag, eating a bowl of spaghetti, on the other. It was a great bag. When the Italian government got wind of this, I received a call: Unless the bags were destroyed, there would be no million-dollar subvention. The bags, amusing as they were, had to go. I, however, kept a few of our "million-dollar bags" as collector's items.

This is a
broken heart!

Remember!

Eric Jacobson

Elie Jacobson was the C.E.O. of Dorothée Bis. He is a small man and had a tiny car to match. At one point, I tried to get into his little car—he was going to drive us around. In those days, I always carried an attaché case, so I'm dropping the case while I'm trying to figure out how I'll fit into the car. Elie was one of the first generation of ready-to-wear designers, starting in the mid-1960s. Although the sketch is set in Paris, I believe he included Le Train Bleu, Bloomingdale's elegant restaurant, to remind me that we had lunch there.

P. O'BRIEN '92

H. TRAUB AND HIS LA

IES!

This is a great sketch of the front row at the Paris collections. I think I'm smiling, surrounded by the powers of the fashion world—Bernardine Morris, Suzy Menkes, Carrie Donovan, and Anna Wintour. The ladies look somewhat unhappy because whatever the show, it was probably an hour late. The objective of the runway show is press and publicity aimed at helping to sell the brand. The excitement and hype is all part of the marketing process. Actually, the buyers get to see the collection weeks before and write their orders then. After the show, the buyers may add a few styles that were created for the show. The pattern is the same in New York, Milan, London, and Paris, with crowds, press, and excitement. It's a crazy system, but it works.

Christian Dior

40ᵉ ANNIVERSAIRE 1987

November 8th-14th

Always, the name Dior will evoke the phrase that rocked the world of 1947.

"The New Look".

Forever changing the course of fashion, the House of Dior set forth a

feminine ideal of elegance and grace lost in the strictures of a World War II economy.

Now, on its 40th anniversary, the luxury, style and exquisite taste that

have come to mean Dior have never been more apparent, more modern. And today,

Bloomingdale's launches a week-long celebration featuring previews of new Dior Collections,

a wealth of Dior designs created exclusively for us, and exciting events throughout every store.

• In honor of the 40th Anniversary of the House of Dior, many Dior designs have been created exclusively for Bloomingdale's. We proudly introduce the first Dior tabletop settings and exclusive bedroom ensembles. A stunning evening gown, luxurious lingerie, coats, a men's dress shirt collection, all exclusive introductions. Come see the new Dior styles in virtually every area of the store.

• Poison, the seductive new fragrance from Christian Dior, in an exclusive deluxe miniature edition, is part of a very special offer during Dior Week at Bloomingdale's. Now, with a Dior purchase in any area of the store, this .3 oz. bottle in its faux malachite and black lacquer box will be priced at just 12.50.

bloomingdale's

Dear Marvin,

My best wishes to one of Christian Dior's true partners and friends.

I hope that we will have another partnership project for Dior's fiftieth anniversary!

With my best personal regards

Bernard Arnault

Today, Bernard Arnault, the chairman of LVMH, is a dominant figure in global luxury and fashion. This is the ad Bloomingdale's had done for the fortieth anniversary of Christian Dior. In the 1980s, when LVMH acquired Lacroix, he negotiated with me about whether Bloomingdale's should carry Lacroix. He was clearly interested in every detail. I was not only a partner for Dior, but an old friend, as my father was the first Dior licensee in America. My dad went to France, negotiated with Jacques Rouet, and returned with the license for Dior intimate apparel. LVMH has had extraordinary growth in the global luxury business in the fourteen years since this letter was written. According to *Forbes*, in 2007, Bernard Arnault is the wealthiest person in France and the 13th wealthiest in the world.

Marvin Traub is a fashion industry legend. He revolutionized modern merchandising in a way that has signifcantly influenced so many in the industry, including myself. In so doing, he put Bloomingdale's on the map as a fashion destination.

Giorgio Armani

Creative Giorgio Armani with his gift for understatement signed a design from his first women's collection, launched at Bloomingdale's in spring 1977. I have great respect for Mr. Armani and how everything he does is in the best of taste. At one point in the early seventies, he and his partner, Sergio Galeotti, invited Lee and me and two of our children to his apartment for lunch (we were vacationing in Milan). The entire decor, as I recall, was in shades of blue, including the risotto. At that lunch, he and Sergio outlined their future strategy in five-year increments—add ready-to-wear, accessories, create a second line, open retail stores, create a fragrance, add home—and it all happened as scheduled. Around the same time, Armani sent me a case of Gavi di Gavi for Christmas, which I immediately returned to him with a thank-you note. I promptly got a phone call from Gabriella Forte, his managing director. "Marvin, I'm sure you don't want to insult Mr. Armani. When he sends you a case of his favorite wine, you accept it graciously." I realized she was probably correct in spite of Bloomingdale's policy regarding gifts. I checked the price of a case of Gavi di Gavi and sent him a boxed set of antique fish knives, costing slightly more, so I could comfortably accept the wine. Incidentally, it was great, and Lee and I still enjoy Gavi di Gavi.

THE BEGINNINGS OF A NEW CONSULTING CAREER 1992–1995

In the fall of 1991, with Bloomingdale's behind me, I had no specific idea of what I would be doing. I knew I wanted to continue working, and I let it evolve from there. I believed—and still believe—that as long as I'm busy, I will stay healthy. I see so many people who leave their jobs, stop working, and immediately seem to get old. I would like to encourage more businessmen and women to enjoy the excitement and commitment of a second career after retiring from their first jobs.

When I left Bloomingdale's, Lee and I traveled as far away as we could go, vacationing in Fiji, Australia, and New Zealand. I returned to work in the Federated corporate offices in December of the same year. But, after three months, it was clear to me that I did not find the corporate environment challenging or rewarding. I was not used to the relaxed nine-to-five atmosphere of the corporate office. It seemed dull and routine, particularly after the excitement of a store like Bloomingdale's. At the same time, many people from outside Federated had approached me to work with them. Taking this as a sign, and armed with a large amount of energy and a host of friends in the United States and around the world, I retired from Federated and launched Marvin Traub Associates with my former Bloomingdale's colleague Lester Gribetz as my partner in March 1992.

I had ten years working for the Bloomingdale's buying office in Europe and one exciting phone call from Marvin Traub to become a part of the team to develop international merchandising projects to make Bloomingdale's like no other store in the world! I was charged with discovering the newest designers, the best items for Bloomingdale's labels, interviewing innovative merchants, creative politicians, mixing products and art, and calling Marvin every Sunday night! From then onwards, nothing became impossible for me!

Chantal Rousseau, vice president of Bloomingdale's, Europe

Lester is an absolutely wonderful human being. I had hired him when I was the assistant to Frank Chase, general merchandise manager for home, in 1958. Lester is very bright, very funny, and a very good merchant. With Lester, everyone laughs. He had been very close to me through the years and ultimately became vice-chairman for menswear and home at Bloomingdale's.

As partners in this new venture, we had handsome offices on the forty-fourth floor of Carnegie Hall Tower, from which we had great views of Central Park. Our clients initially included Federated, as well as Ralph Lauren, American Express, Conran's Habitat, Elizabeth Taylor, and Diane von Furstenberg. It was a very exciting time.

Prior to my retirement, I had been working with the Japanese department store Tokyu to bring Bloomingdale's to Japan. However, my successor at Bloomingdale's, Mike Gould, had other priorities and was not anxious to do a large project in Japan. At that

point, I suggested to the C.E.O. of Federated, Allen Questrom, that I give up Federated as a consulting client and take the option of Japan to Saks Fifth Avenue.

The C.E.O. of Saks Fifth Avenue was Mel Jacobs, an old friend and former executive vice president of Bloomingdale's and president of Federated. Philip Miller, also ex-Bloomingdale's, was president, and Arthur Martinez was C.F.O. They were all interested in taking Saks to Japan. Saks was then owned by Investcorp, a Middle Eastern group, and it, too, agreed that Japan was a good idea, so I contacted the people at Tokyu who had been working with Bloomingdale's.

"I think Saks Fifth Avenue is a good name for Japan," I said. And Tokyu agreed.

To explore this option, we put together a team from Saks that included Nigel French, a British consultant whom I had known for many years. Nigel was very actively involved in Japan. He compiled books on the customs and the practices of the country and the differences between Japanese and American consumers—all aimed at educating our friends at Saks about Japanese culture.

We organized a trip to Japan with Philip Miller and Arthur Martinez to meet with Tokyu and begin discussions. Tokyu had prepared a plan for creating a billion-

dollar business in five locations, but during the negotiations, retail business in Japan began to go into a rapid downward spiral. Although Saks was enthusiastic, when the Japanese market collapsed, Tokyu's investment would have topped one billion dollars, and the company lost interest.

Today, there is a totally different culture in Japan, and I don't know whether Bloomingdale's or Saks would have worked there. In general, the Japanese build bigger stores than Americans do, and they have a very long-term view, with lower profit expectations. They worship global brands. In Japan today, there are ten department stores that do more than $1.2 billion each in sales in their flagship stores. In 2007, Mitsukoshi did $2.5 billion in its Nihonbashi store, and Isetan did $2.3 billion in its Shinjuku store. There's nothing like that in America.

DIANE VON FURSTENBERG AND QVC

Sometimes a deal doesn't work out, as with Saks and Tokyu; however, sometimes the results of a deal far exceed expectations, as did my project with Diane von Furstenberg. Diane is an old friend, and in the early 1990s, she was looking for

The lively Shinjuku Avenue at night in Tokyo, Japan.

ways to sell her product, which had experienced a great boom in the seventies and then slowed down. She'd actually stopped making her famous wrap dress.

"I had lost control of my company and my brand, and I had moved to Paris for a few years," Diane explains. "I came back in the early 1990s and looked at what my brand had become. It was pathetic—most of it had disappeared and what was left was very dusty. I wanted to go back to work, but I didn't know how."

Lester and I talked to Diane about QVC, because we had had some discussions with that company's C.E.O., Doug Briggs.

"One day—I remember it was Saturday, February 29, 1992, because that date happens only every four years—Lester Gribetz, Marvin, Joe Spellman, and I went on a field trip to QVC with the idea of looking at this new concept of retailing," Diane recalls.

We saw the way that it was organized, we met with the announcers, and we became convinced that home shopping and home selling were a great opportunity. At that time, QVC was very anxious to attract recognizable personalities. In the nineties, department stores considered QVC the enemy, because they believed that QVC demeaned, or devalued, the product. This belief is no longer widely held. Sensing its potential, I encouraged negotiations with QVC. While these negotiations were going on, I would often meet with Diane and Barry Diller, then her adviser, now her husband, for Sunday dinner at the Carlyle hotel. Barry, former C.E.O. of Fox, was very impatient with QVC.

"Why are we bothering with this?" he complained. "This is minor-league stuff. Let's go buy NBC, and we'll put Diane's products on NBC."

"You may be right," I reassured him, "but this is like starting in the minor leagues in baseball or like taking a show on the road. Let's first see if we can make it work with QVC."

At that point, Diane had no collection. However, we finalized the deal with QVC and were able to introduce her to a number of people to manufacture the collection she would design. Understandably, Diane wanted to control her collection, and so

Diane von Furstenberg atop the Empire State Building.

Barry had a meeting with Joe, Lester and me.

"We want to control Diane 100 percent. We'd like to buy you out," Barry offered.

So we sold out to Barry for a nominal amount and Diane went on QVC. It was the beginning of her company's resurgence and it was the beginning of Barry's new business—as his interest in QVC had been piqued.

"It was amazing—in two hours we sold $1.3 million [worth of clothing]—it was quite something and exhilarating," Diane recalls. "It turned out to be history. All that success gave me confidence again and got me started. It was a turning point for me, and it was a huge turning point for my husband, who had just left Fox. For him, it was the seed of his new company."

Barry went on to buy QVC, then sold QVC and bought HSN, which is now part of his InterActiveCorp. Diane has gone back into business, and it's much better in its second iteration. Hers is a $200 million-plus business today, and she's really at the height of her influence.

"The QVC thing allowed me to make money, which was nice, and it made me feel secure again," Diane says. "I went from a has-been to a pioneer, and it gave me confidence."

Diane von Furstenberg and her husband, Barry Diller.

as a lion of Retail... He brought show business to Retail and while he was there, made Bloomingdale's the most exciting place to shop.

Diane von Furstenberg

Today, Diane appeals to a young, hip customer, and she is the president of the Council of Fashion Designers of America.

After that, I advised QVC, and Doug Briggs, the C.E.O., told me that QVC had never been very successful at selling books, even with big names like Barbara Taylor Bradford.

"Instead of just selling her book and having her make an appearance, why don't you have her agree to autograph every copy that's sold on QVC?" I suggested.

So they did, and in thirty minutes, she sold four thousand copies of her book—so many that she had to get a machine to help sign them. When I went on QVC one Sunday night to sell my first book, *Like No Other Store,* I sold nine hundred copies in about fifteen minutes—a good number. But I also got to see what it's like to watch an indicator of the sales calls coming in and to feel the pressure if you don't see the sales tally moving up rapidly. Suffice to say, unlike Bradford, I was able to sign all my books by myself.

CONRAN'S HABITAT

Another venture we poured our energy into involved the U. K.–owned home furnishings chain Habitat. The chain had opened stores in the United States under the name Conran's Habitat as there was already a chain operating in the United States called Habitat, and it threatened to sue. (The new name reflected Sir Terence Conran's involvement in the company when it was founded.)

The company had opened twenty-five stores across the country, but many were losing a great deal of money. Because Conran's Habitat was a part of British Home Stores, the owners didn't want to file for bankruptcy in the United States, so they approached us. I looked very carefully at the company—it was losing substantial amounts of money and didn't have very good leases. But it did have a certain amount of cash and a substantial business.

Lester, experienced investor Ken Lazar, and I formed a partnership to buy what was then a $90 million company, but one that was hemorrhaging money. We offered British Home Stores $1,000 for the company. For that price, we got the stores, the inventory, a fair amount of cash, and the obligation to avoid bankruptcy if possible. We brought in many talented people. We recruited Carl Levine, a former senior vice president for furniture and home at Bloomingdale's and put him in charge of furniture. We brought in Helaine Suval, the talented former merchandise manager for tabletop at Bloomingdale's, to supervise housewares and tabletop. We hired my daughter, Peggy, a former Bloomingdale's merchandise manager, to supervise decorative home. Later we added Jody Bradshaw, a brilliant creative merchant for contemporary furniture.

However, we struggled, and after one year our options were to make a substantial infusion of cash, which still might not turn around the stores; file for bankruptcy, which I had originally said that we would not do; or close down the business, sell the most attractive leases, and pay everyone off. The best course was to make do with what we had and close while we could still meet all our obligations. Ken negotiated to sell the leases, and we sold six to Barnes & Noble for $10 million. We took the money, paid off all the creditors, shut down the company, and walked away. So in the end, considering our investment, we did fine.

The lesson I learned was that some businesses, particularly those with very expensive leases, are not likely to work even if you throw enormous talent at them. You can improve them but not necessarily make enough progress to make them successful. Conran's Habitat had an occupancy cost of more than 25 percent, when it should have been 10 to 12 percent.

It was sobering for me, because at that point I thought Lester, Helene, Carl, Peggy, and I could do anything in retail. I was shocked, but nobody was hurt. We walked away with considerably more than our $1,000 investment.

ELIZABETH TAYLOR

When I started my second career, Lester and I worked with Joe Spellman, the guru of the cosmetics industry. Joe and I had originally worked together when he was the executive vice president of Elizabeth Arden and we planned promotions for

The fall and Christmas 1993 catalogs for Conran's Habitat—we did television commercials as well.

Bloomingdale's. He brought Karl Lagerfeld and Elizabeth Taylor and many other designers to Arden and then became a consultant to Estée Lauder. I enjoy working with Joe—he is one of the jolliest, happiest individuals I've ever met—he always hugs people and is forever wearing an infectious grin.

One of the first projects he came to us with was Elizabeth Taylor. He'd worked with her on her fragrance, and now she wanted to license her name for a costume jewelry collection.

"She would like us to meet with her at her home in Bel Air," Joe said.

So we flew out to meet her and drove up to her home. A large Cadillac sat in the driveway. We were ushered into the living room, which was filled with all sizes and shapes of amethyst, and as I recall a Van Gogh, a Monet, and a Manet. We waited almost an hour, and finally, Elizabeth, looking beautiful, came down the stairs wearing a caftan.

Joe whispered to me, "You know why she's been an hour? The Cadillac belongs to her makeup guy." She wouldn't come down until she was beautiful.

Elizabeth sat next to Joe and put her head on his shoulder. "I love this man. I think I have a wonderful jewelry collection, and I'd like to have a jewelry license," she said. "I know you're the right people, but don't come back without $5 million. Get $5 million, and I'm interested." Then she offered, "Can I show you around?"

It was a nice house—an elaborately decorated split-level, but it was not that unique—and outside, there was a fellow in a white T-shirt mowing the lawn.

"Meet my husband," Taylor said. "Larry, come over here."

And Larry Fortensky, Elizabeth's seventh husband, joined us.

Then she took us to her garage. "See those two purple Harley-Davidsons? They're matching ones," Taylor said. "Malcolm Forbes gave one to Larry and one to me. People don't know it, but I put on a helmet and I get on behind him. We go around the neighborhood."

After our meeting, I contacted Jim Preston, the C.E.O. of Avon, which has a large costume jewelry business.

"Jim, how would you like to do Elizabeth Taylor's jewelry?"

Portrait of Elizabeth Taylor.

"I think it's a great idea," he said.

And then I dropped the bombshell. "There's one small problem—Elizabeth won't talk for less than $5 million."

Avon is a multibillion-dollar company, and we were able to negotiate $1 million a year for five years, plus our fee, which was another $1 million, split four ways. Avon set out to work with Elizabeth. The company made copies of her jewelry collection, priced from $50 to $500, but they didn't sell—they were too expensive for the Avon customer. Avon made the jewelry for two seasons, paid Elizabeth, and dropped the project.

We talked about taking her to QVC, but I think that timing is very important in business. This was 1995, and Elizabeth was no longer making movies. It would be difficult to manage a similar deal today

PARTING COMPANY

It had been a whirlwind two years, but at some point in 1994, Lester approached me.

"Marvin, you and I are good friends. I thought when we left Bloomingdale's, we would have a relaxing time. I'm working the same schedule or harder than I did at Bloomingdale's," he said, adding that he wanted to take some time off, so we agreed to part. We had achieved a great start, but I undestood Lester.

What next? I felt it was time to join forces with someone else yet keep my own successful consulting business. Gilbert Harrison, whom I had known many years, seemed a logical candidate.

There is a whole generation of current or former Bloomingdale's alumni who owe part or most of their career success to their exposure to Marvin Traub. The wonderful part of this personal odyssey is that through every phase, Marvin and Lee's friendship with Sheila and me was always consistent, warm, and supportive . amd if you were once one of his people, you were always one of his people. I will always marvel at his never-ending appetite for new discoveries, his indefatigable energy, and his uncanny ability to reinvent his career path so successfully. While others may choose to gracefully retire to the sidelines, Marvin is thriving on setting his career bar even higher and is having a "ball" in the process and usually on only five hours of sleep per night. What a phenomenon he is!!!

Arnold Aronson, former chairman of Saks Fifth Avenue

Marvin Traub has a relentless passion for succeeding, "staying in the game," and for being relevant at all times. Over many decades he has continually updated his perspective, never relying on a historic look backwards; always "in the moment" and forward thinking. He has an energy level that is tireless, keeping everyone around him in a constant "keep up" mode, setting a pace that people half his age would find difficult to maintain. For me, he has set a standard of excellence and achievement that drives my thinking. He has been a boss, mentor, and friend; all of which has helped shape my career. I, like everyone he has touched, am better having had the privilege to know him.

Jeff Sherman, Polo Ralph Lauren

LEARNING TO BE
AN INVESTMENT BANKER:
THE FINANCO YEARS, 1995–2004

For a number of years, even while I was at Bloomingdale's, I had extensive conversations with Gilbert Harrison, an investment banker from Philadelphia. Gilbert was anxious that we find some way to partner. In fact, at the time, B. Altman was for sale, and we had serious discussions about working together on that project.

Gilbert had begun his career as a lawyer and then discovered that the people who were doing financial transactions were making much more money than lawyers. That intrigued Gilbert, so he reinvented himself as an investment banker. He started a company in Philadelphia called Financo. His first transaction was with the Liebeskinds, who had founded Ann Taylor, which Gilbert sold. He did a series of other financial transactions under the Financo banner, then sold his company to Lehman Brothers and moved to New York as a partner. After two years, Lehman Brothers decided to spin off Financo, so Gilbert bought it back from them and went into partnership with Victor Barnett, whose family owned a substantial piece of Great Universal Stores, a parent company of Burberry.

In late 1994, Gilbert and I reached an understanding that I would wear three hats in our partnership. One, for financial transactions that were purely Financo, I would serve as an adviser; two, I would share some consulting projects and deals with Financo; and three, I would oversee my own transactions, since Marvin Traub Associates would continue to exist both for consulting and financial deals. This was a good compromise: to keep my own business yet become part of a larger financial world. I had interviewed with a number of financial firms before settling on Financo. Gilbert was bright, aggressive, and outgoing, with a certain amount of charm. I was convinced that if the shoe-shine stand on the corner were for sale, Gilbert would want to do the deal.

After several years, Gilbert and I developed Financo Global Consulting to broaden the platform of our consulting work. We reached out to executives from the financial and retail industries that included the former chairman of Neiman Marcus, Dick Hauser; the former president of Bergdorf Goodman, Dawn Mello; the former president and C.E.O. of Filene's in Boston and Robinson's-May in Los Angeles, David Mullen; the former president of Fieldcrest-Mills, David Tracy; the former executive vice president of U. S. Shoe, Howard Platt; and many others to create a very impressive roster of consultants.

Gilbert and I agreed that I would share my expertise about the industry with the young people at Financo. He created a large suite of offices for me and when clients came in, we would meet with them together. When he made cold calls, Gilbert found it helpful to say, "I'll bring my partner, Marvin Traub." That seemed to work well for both of us, and in our nine years together, we did a number of exciting transactions.

YUE-SAI KAN

One of the first transactions that Gilbert and I did together was for Yue-Sai Kan. Yue-Sai grew up in China, where her father, Wing-Lin Kan, was a very famous and successful artist. When Bloomingdale's did its promotion of China in 1980, we exhibited and sold his paintings in our art gallery. That was when I first met a very young Yue-Sai.

Yue-Sai moved to New York after getting a degree from Brigham Young University, in Hawaii, and joined her sister, where they ran a business importing Chinese gifts. Yue-Sai also appeared on the local Chinese-language cable television channel. Therefore, when PBS was doing a program on the thirty-fifth anniversary of the People's Republic of China, it was natural for them to ask Yue-Sai if she would go to China as a commentator on the occasion. She accepted the assignment and was an incredible success. Her charm and beauty, combining East and West, was very popular with the young Chinese. So China Central Television (CCTV), the national channel, approached her with an offer.

"Yue-Sai, we'd like you to have your own program on CCTV," they said, and they gave her a one-hour show called *One World.*

Yue-Sai had a wonderful job. She would go to France and call on President François Mitterrand. She'd go to Egypt and visit with President Hosni Mubarak—and ride a camel. She went to India, she met with American presidents, and she traveled all over the world meeting exciting, glamorous people. Being like Yue-Sai became the aspiration of young Chinese women, and she became the most watched personality on CCTV with some three hundred million people tuning in. Yue-Sai had arrived at the top of Chinese television. Young Chinese girls all wanted to grow up to be Yue-Sai. She was very beautiful, very charming, very personable, and one of the most persuasive and practical women I've ever met.

During this time, she was commuting between China and the United States. Her husband, James McManus, was an American marketing guru, and they lived in an

Yue-Sai Kan and her date, Marshall Rose, at our fiftieth anniversary party.

Marvin has been one of the most influential people in my career in countless ways. For more than 25 years, he has encouraged and supported me with my crazy entrepreneurial ideas, enlightened my intellect, clarified my thinking, held my hand when I was in doubt, and opened numerous doors all over the world. Most of all, Marvin has been a mentor and a kind, gentle, and thoughtful friend. I owe him so much!

Yue-Sai Kan

extraordinary, antique-filled townhouse on Sutton Place in New York. With the support of her husband and that of four friends, she set her sights on becoming the Estée Lauder of China. Together, they raised $5 million to start Yue-Sai Kan Cosmetics.

Yue-Sai used all of the Lauder techniques—pricing more moderately than most international brands; getting the best location in each cosmetics department; using gift-with-purchase promotions; and having very well-trained demonstrators, many looking like little Yue-Sais with their traditional bangs. It was a revolution for Chinese cosmetics. In a short time, she was selling in almost one thousand doors.

Her schedule was hectic, however, and she was spending six months of the year or more in China. Consequently, she and Jim divorced—but of course, Yue-Sai kept the townhouse. Gilbert's friend Mort Schrader, a real estate and investing professional with ties to the apparel industry, knew her, as did I, and he let us know that Yue-Sai was anxious to sell her beauty company. When Gilbert and I visited with Yue-Sai in 1996, she gave us a tour of her townhouse but said, "You're too late. I wish I'd met with you sooner. I'm negotiating to sell the company for $30 million."

"What are the sales?" I countered. "About $30 million, and we make a small profit," she said. I said, "Yue-Sai, you can do better than that. Give me a few days to make some phone calls." So I called L'Oréal, Procter & Gamble, and Revlon, and everyone was interested in owning the leading local brand in China. I came back to Yue-Sai and said, "We can probably get you twice that or more. Don't rush to sell the company." She told her advisers she was going to give Gilbert and me the assignment of selling Yue-Sai Kan Cosmetics.

Yue-Sai and I then went on tour. We went to Cincinnati to call on Procter & Gamble. Alan Lafley, who was then president of P&G Asia, was dying to buy Yue-Sai Kan. "We have to buy it," he said. But P&G's C.E.O. was then a very conservative Dutch businessman, Durk Jager. Jager had no interest and waved us off. Lafley, who was later to succeed Jager as head of P&G, called to apologize—he thought they were making a big mistake.

Then we flew to Paris to meet the team from L'Oréal. They wined and dined us, introduced us to all of the senior management, and were ready to bid.

Next, we got a call from Coty: They wanted in.

As the bidding went up, Lauder, Revlon, and other players dropped out. It came down to a bidding competition between Coty and L'Oréal. The C.E.O. of Coty, Peter Harf, was determined to get it. But as negotiations progressed, Yue-Sai became smitten with Gilles Weil, the handsome, debonair Frenchman in charge of international at L'Oréal. She wanted to sell to L'Oréal, but the lawyers and accountants kept giving us more and more requirements. In the meantime, Coty made a flat-out offer of $60 million—double what Yai-Sai's sales had been—and her advisers wanted her to take it. We sold to Coty, which built a new factory in Pudong, China, and began to expand the business.

Well into the process, Yue-Sai was unhappy with the new owners, and L'Oréal was frustrated that it had missed out on the opportunity to acquire the Yue-Sai brand, as I heard from the chairman and C.E.O., Sir Lindsay Owen-Jones.

Three years after Coty bought the company, I seated Yue-Sai next to the then-head of L'Oréal U.S.A., Jean-Paul Agon, at the Financo dinner and let them talk. I called Jean-Paul the next day and told him that L'Oréal was disappointed by the Coty deal, adding that I suspected Coty would be willing to sell. Jean-Paul spoke to Lindsay in Paris. L'Oréal wanted to buy it, and in few months, it acquired Yue-Sai Kan Cosmetics for $120 million. Meanwhile, Yue-Sai still owned 20 percent of the company, so she got a piece of the deal, Financo received two fees, and now Yue-Sai is vice chairman of L'Oréal China, with a factory in Pudong and a growing business.

Yue-Sai continues to be one of the extraordinary figures in international business and is expanding from cosmetics into home furnishings and apparel. She still owns a dominant show on CCTV, *Yue-Sai's World,* which began airing in 2006. Everyone is a friend of Yue-Sai's.

LANVIN

Over the years at Bloomingdale's, I developed great respect for L'Oréal, the largest upscale cosmetic company in the world. In 1988, Lindsay Owen-Jones, an outgoing, bright, and aggressive but polished businessman with the exciting hobby of auto racing, became the C.E.O. for the United States. Subsequently, he became chairman and C.E.O. of L'Oréal worldwide and gave up auto racing at the board's request. At that time, L'Oréal had acquired the designer brand Lanvin as an investment but didn't quite know what to do with it. After a discussion with Lindsay, L'Oréal retained me to work on the brand, reporting to Gilles Weil, who headed international.

Lanvin, founded in 1889, was one of the first French fashion houses. The company boasted two beautiful buildings on the rue de Faubourg Saint-Honoré. Over the years, Lanvin had enlisted various designers for men's and women's collections. In all, there were some fifty stores around the world—some good, some poor, such as the store in London.

I hired Jean-Manuel Pourquet to run the business in America, and we sold the collection to Barneys, Nordstrom, and Bergdorf Goodman, but this wasn't successful enough. After working on the project for three years, I wrote a letter to Gilles Weil suggesting that they either invest a great deal of money in Lanvin or sell it. I argued for selling it, and they did—L'Oréal put it on the market in 2001.

I tried to buy Lanvin with Bear Stearns and Andrew Grossman, who had been president of Jones Apparel, and later C.E.O. of Giorgio Armani, but that didn't work out. I next called Jil Sander, who had left her namesake company by then. She expressed interest in buying it and becoming the designer, but it was too late. L'Oréal had already made a deal with Harmonie S. A., headed by Shaw-Lan Wang, a Taiwanese media magnate, and at the same time, recruited designer Alber Elbaz, who brought chicness and excitement to the Lanvin brand. With Elbaz at the helm, it has gained worldwide recognition and restored luster to the Lanvin brand.

The headquarters of Lanvin, located at 15 and 22 Faubourg Saint-Honoré in Paris.

JOHNNIE WALKER

In the spring of 1996, the management of Johnnie Walker U.S.A. approached us with an interesting assignment: Could we develop Johnnie Walker as a brand? The management's objective was to be able to promote the brand on television, which they could not do selling only scotch. I assured them it could be done and assembled a strong team. I recruited Patrick Guadagno, the former vice president of sales at Armani U.S.A., to run it, and Jeffrey Banks, a well-known designer who trained with Ralph Lauren, to design and source it. Within six months, we produced an apparel collection in China and developed a watch line with Fossil. We then sold the collection to Macy's West, which built a Johnnie Walker shop at its San Francisco store.

Next, we approached NBC, who agreed to accept commercials only if we called it The Johnnie Walker Collection. We filmed our first commercials in Scotland—on a golf course, naturally—and I thought they were great. We felt that the next step was to retain our own professional golfer. We negotiated with the PGA and had a memorable lunch with Jim Furyk and his agent. Jim is an attractive golf pro from Pittsburgh. We learned that when you retain a golf pro, you can buy his hat, his left sleeve, his left pocket or the back of his shirt for logo placement. We opted for them all and agreed on a fee slightly north of $1 million.

We then created a collection of knit shirts just for Jim with a large Johnnie Walker symbol and waited to see it on television. Of course, this was the year that Jim did not win a single tournament. We did catch occasional glimpses of him on the circuit. The next year, with a somewhat different payment schedule, Jim played on the Ryder Cup team, and Lee and I had a chance to to see him play in Brookline, Massachusetts. During this entire period, Jim talked about giving me golf lessons, which I needed desperately, but it never worked out.

Just as our distribution grew and we added Bloomingdale's, the management of Johnnie Walker changed. The new executives felt that they had no business selling apparel. Thus ended our brief journey with Johnnie Walker. Oh well. As Johnnie says, "Keep walking." I still wear my Johnnie Walker watch.

IBEAUTY

In the spring of 1997, Nicholas Berggruen, a friend who combined a family art gallery with investing, invited me to his office to meet a well-known and successful doctor and entrepreneur named Samuel Waksal. Sam said he was a trained researcher and a Ph.D. who had started a public company called ImClone Systems that was working on a cure for colon and rectal cancer. According to him, the drug was an effective cure and was in the testing phase.

Sam had also acquired an Internet beauty company, iBeauty, which sold branded cosmetics online, from the founders, Herman and Jack Jacobs, who retained a substantial interest and continued to warehouse the products. The company had obtained financing from the Tisch family and their representative Helly Weinberger was on the board, as was Sam's friend Martha Stewart. Sam wanted me to join them on the board and serve as a consultant to iBeauty. It was an unusual combination but a tempting offer. I had been considering joining the board of the cosmetics retailer Gloss.com, but it was based rather inconveniently on the West Coast. The Internet seemed the wave of the future, and I agreed.

Our first board meeting, held a few weeks later in the Tisch offices, was unique. Sam presided, and Nicholas, Helly, and the Jacobs brothers were there. Martha arrived fifteen minutes late, bubbling with cheer and carrying a tray of freshly baked danish. The danish were considerably better than the numbers; the company needed growth to become profitable.

In the next few weeks we hired Shirley Lord, a *Vogue* beauty and health editor, to write for us and, with my support, Sam recruited Gabriella Forte, a well-known senior manager who had held key positions at Giorgio Armani and Calvin Klein. Gabriella and I quickly became allies as Sam kept disappearing to fly all over the world, working out deals. Sam maintained a glamorous lifestyle. He had a loft in SoHo where he gave elaborate social parties and held music recitals. Distinguished guests always dropped in, including his good friend Martha.

However, troubles at iBeauty mounted. Sam assured us that ImClone would eventually be worth billions, and I did buy some stock. Meanwhile, Gabriella, Shirley, and I were having difficulty getting paid. Critical to the success of ImClone was gaining U.S. Food and Drug Administration approval to go from the testing to the actual production phase. The price of the stock had soared, but it all unraveled. The F.D.A. did not give its approval to move forward. But before the news came out, Sam sold substantial amounts of stock, and Martha sold some of hers as well. In the resulting fallout, as is now common knowledge, Sam was sentenced to seven years in jail, Martha served time, and iBeauty shut down and was eventually taken over by new management.

In truth, when I first described this research scientist and doctor turned entrepreneur with a medical-research company and a beauty investment company, Lee was very skeptical—even more so after attending some of his glamorous parties. Interestingly, ImClone has had some success in treating colorectal cancer, and the newly restructured company is going forward.

As a further postscript, the Jacobs brothers, always a reserved duo, owned a great deal of inventory beyond iBeauty. Their own company supplied gray market cosmetics to many retailers, including Wal-Mart, but was struggling. Their company carried a very large inventory, and there were reports questioning whether the inventory accounting was correct. Before it could be inspected, the warehouse burned down and the brothers made substantial insurance claims. The brothers were subsequently indicted and sentenced. And all of this comes under the heading "An Interesting Experience."

SHANGHAI TANG

It was rare, of course, for our ventures to end in scandal. Most commonly, we worked with retail groups and launched products and stores. Such was our work with Sir David Tang. An impressive entrepreneur, David owned the Cuban cigar monopoly for Hong Kong and Asia and has a store in the Mandarin Oriental hotel in Hong Kong

David Tang was a gracious, debonair host when Gilbert, Shelly, Lee, and I visited Hong Kong.

that did more than $8,000 a square foot selling Cuban cigars. Once a year, he went to Havana at Fidel Castro's invitation for a conference of Cuban cigar distributors. Not content to limit himself solely to cigars, David started a fine restaurant in Hong Kong called the China Club, now the best place in the city to see and be seen—if you are allowed to join. He opened a China Club in Shanghai as well.

David is the ultimate man-about-town; he dated beautiful women and boasts impressive connections. His grandfather Sir Tang Shiu-kin was a well-known Hong Kong philanthropist and an enormously influential man. And one day, David invited me to help his friend "Sarah" celebrate her birthday at Cipriani in New York; I sat next to her. It was only when the photographers stopped taking pictures that I discovered that Sarah was Sarah Ferguson, the Duchess of York, and one of David's buddies.

In addition to David's cigar and restaurant businesses, he started a retail business in Hong Kong called Shanghai Tang, which sells amusing, updated Chinese products—such as watches with Chairman Mao faces and waving arms, People's Liberation Army hats, peasant blouses, and beautiful silk and velvet jackets. The store feels straight out

Shanghai Tang products were imaginative and fun.

of a Charlie Chan movie (I'm dating myself), with retro art deco decor set in the heart of Hong Kong. The business does very well in the city, both with the locals and the visitors who want to bring home unique gifts.

My work with David began when Shanghai Tang received an infusion of capital from Richemont, the luxury goods group that owns Cartier. David wanted to open a proper store in New York. Of course, David has an overwhelming personality with an ego to match. If he was going to open a store in Manhattan, it would have to be one that would dazzle the locals. David retained Financo and me, and we found a location on Sixtieth Street and Madison Avenue—a twelve-thousand-square-foot store, six times the size of his store in Hong Kong, with twenty-eight-foot-high ceilings. David wanted to spend $1,000 a square foot renovating the space, which is a huge outlay. I couldn't make the numbers for a store of that size work out to show a reasonable profit.

"I don't care, Marvin," David said. "Raise the numbers."

He always had a sense of certainty about his opinions. For instance, he sold terrycloth towels and bathrobes in orange, black, and navy.

"Why not white, David?" I asked.

"I don't like white. It's cheaper," he replied. (Because white cloth is not dyed, it is less expensive.)

"But, David, in the United States more than half the business is done in white."

He said, "I don't care. We're not going to carry white." And so we didn't.

To justify the size of the store and the cost of the renovations, we created an overly aggressive business plan. At the same time, we did not change the products for the American market. David wanted to sell in New York exactly what he sold in Hong Kong.

Naturally, David created an enormous buzz about the store prior to its opening in 1997. We hired Harriet Weintraub, who operates a top-flight public relations firm, to run the opening event. She sent out one thousand invitations to a carefully selected list. However, once the invitations were sent out, David invited another thousand or so of his closest friends. The result, on opening night, was klieg lights, Chinese acrobats, and magicians, but no one could get into the store. There was great excitement, but we upset a large number of carefully selected guests.

Once things calmed down, it became clear that the store could not make its inflated sales plan. Richemont grew impatient with David. It gave up the lease, recruited new management, and found a space one-half the size on upper Madison Avenue. Today, Shanghai Tang is in nine cities around the world and is being built up on a much more modest basis. David is no longer part of it, but he created a unique business.

And me? Because opening night required formal Chinese dress, I still have a black velvet Mao jacket with a white silk shirt in my closet. It is beautiful, my only souvenir of Shanghai Tang, and I look forward to the next black-tie Chinese dinner.

MOSCOW'S MERCURY GROUP

In 1999, Patrick Kenny, the president and C.E.O. of my client Drinks America, had been working with a distributor of vodka in Moscow. Through the distributor, he met an interesting entrepreneur starting in the retail business named Alexander

Reebok, and Patrick suggested he speak with me.

Alex, an outgoing man in his thirties, and one of his partners, Leonid Friedland (the kind of Russian you could imagine banging on his desk), came to see me in New York. They wanted a tour of Bloomingdale's, and I obliged. As we walked through Bloomingdale's, we discussed other stores. I casually mentioned that Barneys New York might be for sale. When they inquired about the price, I told them it would go for between $300 million and $400 million. They said they'd think about it, which left me with the impression that they could write a pretty good-sized check.

Leonid Friedland and his other partner, Leonid Strunin (we called them Big Leonid and Little Leonid), had graduated from school in Russia in the mid-1980s, when perestroika was just beginning. The country was dark and dour, and most people were unsmiling and badly dressed. The national drink was a terrible tasting fermented beverage made from bread called kvass. In GUM, the major department store in Moscow, people lined up to buy soap and toilet paper. However, with perestroika, everything changed. Russia went from a communist to a capitalist society practically overnight. Workers were given shares in their companies, and many of those shares were acquired by aggressive oligarchs who bought them for very little. There was enormous economic growth, social change, and the creation of a Russian consumer-driven economy, resulting in a new crop of millionaires and billionaires. In 2008, according to *Forbes*, there were more billionaires in Moscow (38) than any other city in the world. Until perestroika, no luxury brands were interested in Russia, but that all changed in the 1990s.

The two Leonids opened a store that sold Russian gifts and souvenirs in the most "American" hotel in Moscow—the Radisson Hotel. After six months, the Radisson's management approached them.

"We like the two of you, but we really don't like selling Russian souvenirs in the lobby of our hotel. We want to continue your lease, but we'd like you to find something else to sell."

The Leonids decided on jewelry and acquired Chopard for Moscow, a line which took off immediately. Then they opened Bulgari in another shop, followed by Tiffany

In 1986, I was thirty-four years old and had just been promoted to president and C.E.O. of Bullock's Wilshire. On my first visit to Paris for the prêt-à-porter shows in March, 1986, Marvin Traub, the experienced, charismatic C.E.O. of Bloomingdale's, took me under his wing and showed me the ropes about surviving fashion week. This may sound trivial for someone not familiar with the fashion business, but without the endorsement of this highly regarded retail icon, a newcomer like me could barely get a hotel room during fashion week. In fact, when I arrived at the Hotel Crillon, I was told that it was completely sold-out, and I had no reservation. I tried everything to convince them I had a confirmed reservation but they refused to listen until I told them I was traveling with Mr. Traub. Suddenly, a room became available. Not only did Marvin Traub open the door to my hotel room, he opened the door for private audiences with Yves Saint Laurent, Karl Lagerfeld (Chanel), Gianfranco Ferre, Christian Lacroix, and many more of the world's most influential fashion designers. As busy as he was, Marvin always took the time to share his knowledge with the next generation of retailing executives, and for that I am eternally grateful.

Terry Lundgren, chairman and C.E.O. of Macy's Inc.

When Marvin Traub first came to see my collection in 1985, it was as if God had come down from heaven. He said to me, "You could be another Ralph Lauren." I remember his words to this day and will never forget how I felt. Marvin's blessing gave me the confidence I needed. Within a short period of time, we were on fire. It was the beginning of my fashion career. I will forever be grateful to Marvin for understanding and respecting my vision with such incredible support.
Tommy Hilfiger

I met Marvin at the beginning of my career in the fashion industry as a trainee at Bloomingdale's. In the intervening thirty years, I have had the privilege of working closely with this remarkable leader. He is a consummate global businessman and a leading ambassador of the fashion industry. Throughout Marvin's career, he has exhibited a timeless dedication and passion for style, innovation, and the pursuit of excellence. He has been instrumental in the development of the careers of many of our industry leaders today.
Denise V. Seegal, former president & C.E.O, VF Sportswear

& Co. and Rolex in a multibrand store. In a period of two to three years, they became incredibly successful and were the first to recognize luxury jewelry as a great opportunity. In addition, they realized that many wealthy Russians were traveling to Paris, London, and Milan to buy their clothes. They saw an opportunity but didn't know anything about the fashion business. And so they found a Russian woman named Alla Verber to help them.

Alla was born in St. Petersburg but had lived in Canada, where she ran clothing boutiques. She's very charming, very enthusiastic, attractive, dynamic, outgoing, and is one of the most instinctively smart people that I've ever met in the world of fashion. She knows instantly what sells by looking at a line.

Alla was charged with getting Gucci, Giorgio Armani, and the other luxury brands for the Leonids' company, the Mercury Group. She decided to begin with Gucci and secured an appointment with Domenico De Sole, then president and managing director of Gucci, at his offices in London. Alla went out and bought a head-to-toe Gucci outfit, complete with a $5,000 pair of green alligator boots. Domenico was intrigued by her. "If you want Gucci for Russia, you can have it," he

(From left) Europinsky Mall, one of Moscow's newest contemporary shopping centers; David Wells, designer of TsUM, Dick Hauser, Morty Singer, Alla Verber, and me in Red Square; as this sign in Moscow shows, the Mercury Group offers great luxury brands in their *passagen* adjacent to Red Square.

said, and they agreed to open a store together. After Gucci, Alla called on Giorgio Armani in Milan, who today is a big fan of hers. He, too, acquiesced.

While Alla acquired these brands, the Leonids found an apartment building on a main street and converted the entire first floor into a series of boutiques, successfully adding brands like Fendi, Chanel, Brioni, and Dolce & Gabbana.

Their next location was in the heart of Moscow, a *passagen* just one block from the Kremlin that they converted into world-class luxury boutiques for Giorgio Armani, Gucci, Baccarat, Dior, and Yves Saint Laurent, among others.

The Leonids also worked with automotive brands and obtained the Bentley franchise for Moscow. When they opened the showroom in August 2003, their allocation of twenty-four Bentleys—a $300,000 car—sold out in three weeks, an indication of the level of affluence in Moscow. They gave Alla a Bentley as a Christmas bonus, provided she hired a bodyguard to drive it.

Before I began working with the Leonids, their company bought a store in Moscow called TsUM. They invited me to Moscow to see how they could reconstitute TsUM—changing the design, adding designer brands—to make it a modern-day

1. Marvin and Sung-Joo Kim. 2. Phyllis George, Lee, and Marvin. 3. Shireen El-Khatib, the C.E.O of the Luxury Division at Al Tayer. 4. Allen Questrom and Marvin. 5. Alexander Bolen and Oscar de la Renta. 6. Lindsay Owen-Jones 7. Lester Gribetz, Leonard Lauder, and Joe Spellman. 8. Aslaug Magnusdottir, Marvin, and Morty Singer. 9. Patrick Guadagno and Marvin with Johnnie Walker products. 10. Marvin and Gilbert Harrison.

department store. TsUM's 240,000 square feet were well-situated one block from the Bolshoi Theatre, but the store was very old-fashioned. The year before Alex and the Leonids bought it, TsUM did $32 million with two thousand employees, a payroll that Alex and the Leonids cut down to eight hundred employees after owning the company for three months.

When Alla and I were laying out the new store, I asked to see the offices on the sixth floor. I was looking to see where we could get more selling space. I opened the door of one office around noon, and there were three executives resting their heads on their arms, sleeping at their desks.

"Alla, I'm not sure we need all these people," I said, realizing the habits of the old Communist regime were hard to break.

During an eighteen-month period, I visited Moscow frequently, working with Alla and her team. My associate, Morty Singer, and Dick Hauser joined us. We replanned TsUM and added new brands, consulting closely with Alla. A typical working lunch consisted of vast amounts of caviar, smoked salmon, cheese, wonderful fresh breads, and an occasional glass of vodka. I brought home a great deal of caviar as well. Not a bad consulting assignment.

Later, the Mercury Group added a 750,000-square-foot shopping center in Zhukovka, the wealthiest suburb of Russia. They called it the Luxury Village. In it, they have Louis Vuitton, Chanel, Gucci, Ralph Lauren, a great restaurant called Avenue, and Bentley, Maserati, and Harley-Davidson showrooms. Here, Saturday is the busiest retail day. Traffic at the Luxury Village is very light by Western standards, but it is not unusual for one customer to spend $100,000. It does a great deal of business with a relatively small number of customers.

Today, TsUM is doubling in size to 500,000 square feet. It will be the largest upscale store in Eastern Europe—not bad for three guys fresh out of high school who opened a gift shop in the Radisson just sixteen years ago. Today, they head a billion-dollar empire.

RALPH LAUREN IN MOSCOW

Before I started working with the Mercury Group, Alex and the two Leonids invited Roger Farah, president and C.O.O. of Polo Ralph Lauren, to Moscow. As soon as he got off the plane, there were two security men in camouflage suits carrying Kalashnikovs, waiting.

Everywhere Roger went in Moscow, these armed security men went along with him. I believe these men were protecting the Leonids, not just Roger, but all of the security understandably made Roger very uncomfortable. He'd heard—and it is true—that there is a certain amount of violence in Moscow.

"Who needs it?" he said after spending two days there. "I'm not going to open in Russia. We've got too many other places to go."

Six months later, when the Leonids recruited me for TsUM, they told me, "Roger Farah came, and he doesn't want to work with us."

Roger's story was somewhat different, but I was eventually able to convince him to meet Alla Verber. She told him about Gucci, Giorgio Armani, Tiffany, and the other brands she was working with and suggested he come back for a second visit. When Roger returned, there were a couple of fellows in dark suits following him, but they were much more discreet this time.

Roger decided to open in Moscow, but Ralph would not open anything less than a flagship store. I think one of the reasons Ralph thought it was important to have a flagship store in Moscow, aside from it being one of the important world capitals, is that Ralph's family roots go back to Russia. It was important to Ralph that he come to Russia in a style befitting the Polo Ralph Lauren image. They found the perfect location for a flagship store at the head of the *passagen* near the Kremlin in a wonderful, old building across from the Armani store.

It took almost five years to work out the details. There were sixty people from Polo Ralph Lauren in Moscow in May 2007 for the opening of his store. He had a team of people there for four weeks, because Ralph makes sure every detail is perfect. They set up the store, trained the salespeople, oversaw all the display, and

Marvin Traub was just assuming the helm of Bloomingdale's when I was starting my career, and early on we developed a very close working relationship. His receptiveness to what I was doing, whether my first men's ties, my first women's shirts and sportswear, or my first home collection, was incredible. He supported me with great shops that gave me incredible exposure and credibility because by that time, through his talent and leadership, Bloomingdale's had become "the store." Of course, not everything I did was a hit from the beginning; there were bumps in the road. But Marvin's perseverance, commitment, and his tireless energy were always there for me. He was a true partner in helping me build my company and is one of the great merchants.

Ralph Lauren

Marvin Traub and Ralph Lauren at the U.S. embassy in Moscow. Photo by Suzy Menkes.

executed a powerful launch campaign. For the opening night black-tie dinner at the U.S. embassy, the Polo Ralph Lauren team brought tablecloths, centerpieces, decanters, and even new draperies so that the embassy would be appropriate for a Polo Ralph Lauren evening. For Ralph, opening in Russia was a wonderful experience. He had global media coverage and it was very well done. In Russia, Ralph was a rock star. The Russians don't like dressing up in black tie, but for Ralph Lauren they did.

One day, prior to the store's opening, a Russian woman pounded on the front door—she just had to be let in. We relented, and she went to the handbag counter.

"I need five 'Ricky' handbags," she said. Ricky handbags are made of alligator and sell for $20,000 each. "I have to have them before my friends do." She got them.

Ultimately, the Ricky handbag became a status symbol in Moscow, and Polo Ralph Lauren ended up pulling the handbags from its stores all over the world and shipping them to Moscow. Not surprisingly, the store did more than $1 million in its first weekend; and the projected sales for its first year for the two stores will top $20 million.

OSCAR DE LA RENTA

One of the most popular, long-lasting and admired designers in our industry is Oscar de la Renta. He is the epitome of polish and good taste. I've known him for many years.

He's been enormously successful at Bergdorf Goodman, Saks Fifth Avenue and Neiman Marcus. However, if one looks at the most successful brands—Louis Vuitton, Gucci, Hermès, Prada, Polo Ralph Lauren—one thinks of them through their own stores, not only through their wholesale business.

One day, I had a Four Seasons lunch with Oscar and his son-in-law Alex Bolen, who had recently started working at the company. I suggested that they had an enormous opportunity in the retail business.

"Could we make money?" Alex asked.

"Retail should be more profitable than the wholesale business," I explained. They hired me through Financo Consulting to plan and implement their retail strategy. I brought in Dawn Mello as an additional consultant. We put together a plan showing that a Madison Avenue shop with sales of $3.5 million could break even. And if Oscar did trunk shows, at which he is enormously successful, they would really coin money.

In department stores, you sell apparel through apparel departments and accessories through accessories departments. But if you have your own boutique, it is much more important to have shoes, handbags and scarves, to make the store more productive. Dawn improved these categories for Oscar.

We found a great location on Sixty-seventh Street and Madison Avenue—the former Sergio Rossi store. It had a separate raised platform in the back that would be perfect for the long ball gowns for which Oscar is famous. Interestingly, gown sales only account for 11 or 12 percent of Oscar's business. The design firm we hired created an elegant store to match Oscar's personality, complete with coral stone from the Dominican Republic as the backdrop. The windows opened, so you could see into the store. We recruited a store manager from Michael Kors who turned out to be terrific. And when the store opened, instead of doing $3.5 million in the first year, it did almost $7 million. Today, the store does well over $10 million in two thousand square feet.

"Marvin was dead-on when it came to our retail business," Bolen shares. "We had a lot of concerns about opening on Madison Avenue, six or seven blocks north of Bergdorf Goodman, our top wholesale account. But Marvin told us it would be a boon to Bergdorf's just to have the visibility on Madison Avenue— and in fact, he's right. We have had high double-digit growth at Bergdorf's ever since we've opened the Madison Avenue store."

Bolstered by such success, we negotiated for a second store in Bal Harbour, and since then, Oscar has opened up stores on Rodeo Drive and at the Americana Mall in Manhasset, Long Island. Oscar is getting ready to expand to Europe as well, starting in Spain. I believe retail will be an increasingly important part of Oscar's business.

From 1995 to 2004, I wore three hats: I ran my own company, Marvin Traub Associates, I had an advisory role at Financo, and I supervised Financo Global Consulting. While I have great respect for Gilbert Harrison, I began to feel it was time to set up my own company. Truthfully, I was used to being in charge. In addition, the bright young people working for me were anxious for us to grow the business on our own. After considerable negotiation with Gilbert, I decided to leave and brought them to Marvin Traub Associates, along with Amy Hafkin, my office manager and assistant of fourteen years. We moved into offices on Park Avenue and Fifty-fourth Street.

Oscar de la Renta at the CFDA Fashion Awards in 2007.

I very much consider Marvin a mentor. Coming from a finance background, I approach retail with a great amount of trepidation. I'm not sure what the professor would have to say about my grades. He's been a tremendous help to me in learning this business. And moreover, he was dead-on when it came to our retail business.

Alex Bolen, president and C.E.O. of Oscar de la Renta

MTA'S WORLD TOUR:
LEAVING FINANCO ON MY OWN
2004 AND BEYOND

The decision to leave Financo and my partnership with Gilbert Harrison after nine years was a major one not without its risks. I would be on my own, so all expenses would be mine, and at age 78, I was starting a new venture. Gilbert did his best to keep me from going, but I was confident that my team and I could succeed on our own.

At the time I left Financo, I became a senior adviser to Compass Advisers, a financial services company headed by Stephen Waters, a younger compatriot from Harvard Business School who had been cohead of mergers and acquisitions at Morgan Stanley, and then co-C.E.O. of Morgan Stanley Europe. Steve is articulate and smooth. Although he is on the quiet side, when a deal is on the table, he is convincing and passionate. I was to advise Steve and to organize projects for us to work on together. And so, after a brief stint at Park Avenue and Fifty-fourth Street, Marvin Traub Associates moved into the Compass Advisers' offices at Fifty-third Street and Lexington Avenue. This move reflected Steve's addiction to baseball. Our offices overflowed with memorabilia—from Babe Ruth's uniform to George Selkirk's bat, seats from Yankee Stadium, and autographed photos of all the Yankee teams. People loved to visit us just to look at the walls. Almost immediately, we accomplished our first transaction together—when Compass represented Slatkin & Co. and negotiated the sale to Limited Brands.

A major story from the *Calgary Herald* in 2007, when I was working on a real estate project in Calgary, Canada.

An interview with the
RETAIL
ICON

MARIO TONEGUZZI
CALGARY HERALD

Marvin Traub is widely recognized as a retail marketing guru who helped transform the industry in the United States in the 1950s.

Later under his leadership, he propelled **Bloomingdale's** to celebrity status as a fashion trendsetter.

Now, the legendary figure has taken on a new project. He's a consultant for **Deerfoot Meadows**, helping develop the vision for The Village concept, which will likely transform the retail landscape in Calgary for years to come.

"My consulting business is very active globally with clients in Dubai, Athens, Istanbul, Moscow, India," Traub told the Herald this week. in an exclusive interview, during a visit to Calgary to get a feel of the city and the retail industry here.

"I met Ken (Mariash, developer of Deerfoot Meadows) and I was fascinated with the story of Calgary, which, like most Americans, I really didn't fully appreciate what was happening here.

"I realized that an enormous number of retailers globally also don't know what is happening. So Ken and I talked about working together."

They met in New York in December.

That led to Traub's trip to Calgary this past week on a mission to be better acquainted with the local economy and retail market so that in talking to global retailers he is better informed about the environment here.

"It kind of looks to me that Calgary is under-served in the retailing com-

MARVIN TRAUB

- Former CEO and chairman of Bloomingdale's;
- Graduate of the Harvard Business School with Distinction in 1949;
- Started Marvin Traub Associates, consulting firm, in 1994 and today has 30 projects in 12 countries, including the United Kingdom, United Arab Emirates, France, Panama, China, Russia, Greece, Italy, Canada and Lebanon;
- Former vice-chairman and director of Campeau Corporation and a director of Federated Department Stores;
- Recipient of The Gold Medal of the National Retail Federation in 1991;
- Widely regarded as a retail marketing guru and for helping transform the retail industry in the United States in the 1950s.

At this same time, I also became chairman of SD Retail Consulting, formerly Senn-Delaney Management Consultants. I had worked with this company at Bloomingdale's, and it was expert on operations, back of the house, and logistics, so its expertise complemented mine. In the coming years, we worked on a number of projects together. Greg Rubin, an outgoing, savvy businessman, is SD's president and C.E.O., and he and I hit it off immediately.

SD Retail Consulting is a joint venture with Hilco, a multibillion-dollar conglomerate based near Chicago that is a global leader in all forms of valuation of businesses, equipment, and property. It is a major purchaser of distressed assets and owns venture-capital companies that acquire businesses in the United States, the United Kingdom, Europe (Karstadt department stores), and Japan. Hilco is privately owned by Jeffrey Hecktman, an aggressive, tireless international businessman with a passion for deals; we met at a Four Seasons breakfast and became good friends.

The team at Marvin Traub Associates changed. Morty Singer, who had been with me since 2002, became senior vice president, and we added another talented partner, Aslaug Magnusdottir, in 2006.

Morty Singer has a most unusual background. His great-grandfather Isaac Merritt Singer created the Singer Sewing Machine Company. Morty is truly international—his mother is French and his father, Forbes Singer, is American. Morty was raised in the United Kingdom, and he came to the United States to attend the University of Pennsylvania. After graduation, he worked with JPMorgan, headed the American office of Quintessentially, an upscale U. K.–based credit card company, and then joined me at Financo in 2003. He encouraged me to take the company out on our own. Morty is very polished and charming. He loves business and travel, and he has turned out to be an extraordinary support for me in the five years we've worked together. He is rapidly becoming a great merchant and, even more important, I consider him one of the most talented young people I have mentored in my long, fulfilling career—plus he always knows the hot new "in" places and latest trends.

Our newest partner, Aslaug Magnusdottir, is a tall, great-looking, blonde Icelander who formerly chaired the Icelandic Dance Company, trained as a lawyer, and was educated in the United States through a Fulbright at Duke University School of Law and Harvard Business School. Subsequently, she moved to the United Kingdom and, after three years at McKinsey and Company, spent three years in charge of venture capital for an aggressive Icelandic company called Baugur, ultimately overseeing a dozen investments in the United Kingdom. She then married a Harvard Business School classmate, moved to the United States, and joined us. Morty and Aslaug keep me in touch with the changing tastes of our young consumers, as both are a great deal younger than I am. We make a unique team.

The third key member of our team is Amy Hafkin. Amy started as my assistant in 1992 but today manages my business. She is warm, caring, and dedicated. Once on our own, I promoted her to general manager, and she focuses on operations so I can concentrate on consulting and financial transactions. She is a good "right arm" for me.

The rest of our team includes the invaluable Natalie Bozoyan, my assistant, who attends classes in the evenings at Parsons The New School for Design, and John Paterson. John is a most unusual driver. He has been with me for six years and feels he is part of the family, so he joins in on all of the conversations in our car, regardless of the guests. Four years ago, when John married, I gave away his charming Australian bride, Wendy. As our business grew, we added enthusiastic analyst and consultant Kelsey Scroggins, who assists us with our ever-increasing work load

In our work together, it was very evident that in the past decade retailing and consumer goods had become increasingly global. As a result, more and more of our consulting business was developing from various areas of the world, partly through our initiatives and partly through clients who approached us. Although we focused on global projects, we also had some very interesting opportunities domestically. I'll share some of both on the following pages.

1. Marvin with Stanley Marcus. 2. Marvin and former Nebraska senator Bob Kerrey, president of The New School. 3. Lester Gribetz 4. Phyllis George, Marvin, and Lee at the Kentucky Derby. 5. Morty Singer and Marvin Traub. 6. With the Missoni Family—Vittorio, Tai, Lee, Rosita, Angela, and Marvin. 7. Halston, Andy Warhol, Martha Graham, Lee, and Marvin. 8. Marvin Traub and Bill Blass. 9. Marvin Traub and Hubert de Givenchy. 10. Martha Graham, Halston, Hildy Parks, and David Mahoney. Mahoney acquired Halston for J. C. Penney.

THE MIDDLE EAST

I began working in the Middle East with a Wharton School graduate named Mohammad Al-Shaya in 1999. He came to visit me in New York after hearing about my relationship with Financo. He arrived in a well-tailored suit, and after our meeting, invited me to make my first visit to the Middle East. When I got off the plane in Dubai, there was a sea of men waiting on the tarmac wearing long, white outfits—dishdashas—with head coverings. I didn't recognize Al-Shaya. Luckily, he found me, and we went on to visit Kuwait and Dubai. I remember being struck by Dubai's rapid growth. In Kuwait City, I met his family in the corner of his huge family mosque. He took me to the seaside where they were building three fifteen-thousand-square-foot homes—one for each family member. They owned the licenses for Sheraton Hotel Debenhams and Starbucks. That was my initial exposure to the Middle East. Al-Shaya wanted to expand his retail properties beyond the hotel and Starbucks. However, we didn't end up working together.

About six months later, I got a call from Tony Salame, who was building a major store in Beirut. He had heard about me, knew I'd been to Kuwait, and wanted to work with me to plan his store. I was wary about going to Beirut because of its civil war. I didn't know if I wanted to do business in that part of the world and told him so. He asked me to meet him in Venice, and since I was going to be in Italy, I agreed. Tony, who was in his early thirties, turned out to be an attractive, outgoing, strong, creative merchant from the Christian minority in Lebanon. He assured me that I would really enjoy Beirut. He said it is the "Paris of the Middle East." He wanted to build a 75,000-square-foot store, on the model of Barneys New York. It sounded like an exciting project. I liked him and agreed to work with him.

Lee and I flew to Beirut in July 2000. It had been recovering from fifteen years of civil war, and in order to redevelop the city, fifteen acres of seaside had been filled in, creating a handsome new downtown of buildings, shopping centers, nightclubs, and cafés. The first day, I toured the city, the downtown, the site for the new store, and saw Tony's many boutiques. Later that evening, Tony held a dinner in our honor for two

The Jumeirah Emirates Towers in Dubai, United Arab Emirates. I usually stay at this hotel.

hundred guests on the roof of the Intercontinental Phoenicia Beirut Hotel. There was music, dancing and a very elaborate dinner. People were beautifully dressed. Fifteen minutes into dinner, Tony took the microphone.

"I'm very pleased that Mr. and Mrs. Traub are here," he said. "Marvin is the former head of Bloomingdale's, and he is working on my project. Marvin, would you say a few words?"

I wasn't prepared, but I spoke about how Beirut had some of the most beautiful women in the world, as well as some of the friendliest people—both true. I went on: "I didn't know what to expect but was impressed by the rebuilding and by the positive attitude the Lebanese have toward the United States. I think most Americans treat the Middle East as if it's one pot—they don't understand that Lebanon is different from Iraq, Iran, and other countries. Somehow, you should make other Americans besides me understand what's going on."

After I sat down, Fouad Siniora, then minister of finance, who was sitting at my table, asked to speak with me. We took our wineglasses and went out to the lobby. "I was very impressed with what you said, and I'd like you to meet the prime minister. I'd like you to say the same thing to him because you might get him to do something. Would you do that?" he asked. "Sure, when should we meet?" "How's tomorrow? Come to the presidential palace. I'll introduce you to Prime Minister Hariri."

Rafik Hariri was a very successful developer from Lebanon. He founded a company called Solidere that funded the renovation and rebuilding of the city after the war—a $2 billion project—and he was a strong proponent of the independence of Lebanon.

I met with the prime minister and repeated what I'd said at the dinner. "People in the United States think that Lebanon is dominated by the Syrians," I stressed.

"That is my problem, and we are trying to solve it because we have to do it," Hariri said. "Can you help us find the right public relations agency in the United States and get our story across?"

He asked me to convey the message to the acting American ambassador, as well, which I did, though Hariri never followed up. Less than two years later, he was assassinated in front of the Intercontinental Phoenicia—the very hotel at which I had made my impromptu speech. The new prime minister is my friend Fouad Siniora. I fear for him as well—it is still a difficult part of the world.

I enjoyed working with Tony. We planned the store with larger cosmetics, shoe, and handbag areas because in that part of the world all women use those products regardless of how they dress. When it opened, it was hugely successful. We got to know Tony and his wife, Elham, very well and we vacationed together when visiting Lebanon. Once, on a trip to the north, Lee casually asked, "Is there any danger here?"

"Well, you're in the middle of Hezbollah country," Tony said. "You see over there—that tower? That was hit by Israeli artillery last week, but we'll be fine."

After the store was open, Tony invited me to join him in Dubai—he felt that was where the action was going to be. He set up a meeting with the president of the Dubai Chamber of Commerce, Obaid Al Tayer. We talked together about what was happening in Dubai and, clearly, this was the center of the action. That evening, we had dinner with a cousin of the sheik's who was developing a shopping center. He wanted to meet privately, so we could "enjoy the best Peking duck in the region" prepared by his private Chinese chef, recruited from Beijing. Our host was looking very chic in a black silk shirt, discussing his horse farm in Kentucky. Tony was thinking of opening a store in his shopping center, unusual in that the Wafi Center is built in the image of Egypt at the time of the pharaohs. But nothing came of the meeting.

However, after I returned to the United States, Obaid Al Tayer asked if he could meet with me in New York to disuss his ventures. He had a very successful chain of boutiques—Giorgio Armani, Yves Saint Laurent, Bottega Veneta, and Bulgari, among others—but he wanted a department store.

"And I think you can help me," he said. "Of all the stores in London, Harvey Nichols has the highest percentage of shoppers from the Gulf. I would like to own the name Harvey Nichols for Dubai and the Gulf. Once we get that, I need your help in planning the store."

Because I knew Dickson Poon, who owns and is the chairman of Harvey Nichols, and I knew Joseph Wan, the C.E.O. of Harvey Nichols London, it was very easy for me to contact them. By law, there has to be local ownership in Dubai, and Harvey Nichols had a strategy of leasing its name to local partners, which it had already been done in Riyadh, Saudi Arabia. We began a very long period of negotiation. Dickson Poon's group can be very tough, so it took six months of traveling between New York, Dubai, and London, but we finally reached a deal for a ten-year license and a ten-year renewal.

I enjoy working with Obaid. He went to college in Colorado, is a great businessman, and was very smart, very pleasant, very creative, and very ambitious about what he wanted to achieve. Obaid appointed Shireen El-Khatib, who had been supervising all of the luxury boutiques, to run Harvey Nichols Dubai. Shireen is not a native of Dubai, she has a Palestinian father and an Egyptian mother. She is bright, very capable, and intense. She wears Western clothes and accessories and frequently wears jeans to work. Like many people from the Middle East, she is an avid smoker and is always saying, "Marvin, excuse me, I have to go smoke." She has been with Obaid for twelve years and seen his business grow to a multibillion-dollar global company. This past year, she was promoted to C.E.O. of Al Tayer Insignia, the luxury-brand division that includes Harvey Nichols Dubai.

Shireen and I selected a West Coast–based architectural firm, Callison, and planned the store with Martin Anderson, a principal with that firm. To create a facade reminiscent of Harvey Nichols London, we replicated the clock that's a fixture in front of the London store. We laid out the store quite differently from what had been done elsewhere in the Middle East, striving for a contemporary feeling, using wider aisles and very good lighting. We planned the organization and recruited Eda Kuloglu, a top-flight merchant from the Beyman department store in Istanbul. I approached the Lauders—William and Leonard—to help lay out the cosmetics department. In exchange, they gave us MAC (we would be the first department store to carry MAC in Dubai), La Mer, and Bobbi Brown, as well as Estée Lauder and Clinique. Obaid has his own cosmetics retail and distribution company called Areej, which is the distributor of Guerlain and other brands. The staff running Areej also run the cosmetics division at Harvey Nichols Dubai, as well as twenty retail stores, and are very professional.

We started with a blank sheet of paper and ended end up with a concept for a 130,000-square-foot department store and a team to run it. We now have what is undoubtedly the most successful department store in the Middle East and are contemplating opening additional stores in other parts of the region.

Prior to my joining Obaid and Shireen, the European brands were established in the Middle East. The Al Tayer Group was working with Giorgio Armani, Gucci, Bottega Veneta, and adding such brands as Ozwald Boateng, Matthew Williamson, and Emilio Pucci. I introduced the idea of the new generation of contemporary brands that were succeeding in America but that had not yet come to the Middle East, such as Juicy Couture, Elie Tahari, Tory Burch, Diane von Furstenberg, Brooks Brothers, Michael Kors, and Oscar de la Renta—brands which became successful very rapidly.

Although Polo Ralph Lauren was licensed to someone else in the Gulf, it was only for apparel and accessories, so I arranged for Harvey Nichols Dubai to become the Ralph Lauren home furnishings licensee for the Gulf. We opened a thirty-five-hundred-square-foot Ralph Lauren Home shop, which turned out to be very successful, as Dubaians bought entire rooms of Ralph Lauren furniture. We planned the store for about $40 million, and in the first year, it did almost $90 million. Today, it does substantially more.

Obaid has an extraordinary multibillion-dollar company. It publishes *Gulf News*, the leading English daily newspaper of the Gulf, and *Friday*, a weekly family magazine with the largest circulation in the region. Al Tayer Motors has the second-largest Land Rover distributorship in the world, the fourth-largest

Ford/Lincoln dealership in the world, and the largest Maserati and Ferrari dealerships in the Middle East.

As frequently happens with people I'm doing business with, we've become good friends. Obaid even flew to New York to help celebrate my birthday. In Dubai, Obaid likes me to join him at his beach club at the end of the day, have a wonderful dinner, share ideas, and talk about Middle Eastern politics. For me, that is part of the fun of what I do. Ours has grown beyond a business relationship—I care about him; he cares about me—even though we're clearly of very different backgrounds. I'm very fortunate to have Tony Salame in Beirut, Obaid Al Tayer, Shireen, and the team in Dubai, Alla Verber in Moscow, Constantin Lambropolous in Athens, and the Tatas in India, whom I'll discuss later in this chapter.

Because I'm looking at retailing globally, having had accounts like the Mercury Group and Al Tayer is helpful as I look at the rest of the world. It's important to know which lines work best overscas.

The Al Tayer Group is comprised of five brothers, and two years ago, Obaid's nephew, Khalid Al Tayer, whose father is a highly regarded public servant, joined the company. Khalid is thin and very intense. He was educated at Babson College in Massachusetts and worked for three years at McKinsey in the Middle East with Aslaug Magnusdottir, one of my partners. Khalid makes a very good impression and, at 29, has climbed six of the seven tallest mountains in the world—and has a bad knee to show for it.

Khalid is in charge of strategic planning and new business development. After Khalid joined the company, it became two separate divisions: one for the strong luxury business and another for the middle-range lifestyle business, which includes stores such as the Gap and represents a very large opportunity for future growth. Indeed, the Al Tayer Group has grown fivefold since I began working with it in 2002. I'm confident that in the next few years, it will become a global retail power.

Marvin altered the trajectory of my career on several oc-
casions. His mentorship was invaluable to my success as publisher of Men's Health magazine beginning in 1992. In 1999,
he introduced me to Ralph Lauren, which in turn lead to my
own "second career" in luxury fashion marketing and product
licensing at Polo Ralph Lauren. Marvin's passion for business,
his work ethic, (not to mention his air travel endurance and
unyielding schedule), his persistent curiosity and innate opti-
mism continue to inspire me.
Jeff Morgan, president of Product Licensing, Polo Ralph Lauren

Khalid Al Tayer, Mike Gould, C.E.O of Bloomingdale's, me, and Tony Spring, new Bloomingdale's president, in the
lobby of the world-famous Burj Al Arab Hotel in Dubai.

CHINA

We met another interesting personality through Phyllis George, the former Miss America. Phyllis and I had been good friends for twenty years. We went to the Kentucky Derby when her ex-husband, John Y. Brown, Jr., was governor of Kentucky and Bloomingdale's was working on a promotion of Kentucky crafts.

In 2005, Phyllis introduced me to a Chinese entrepreneur named Miles Kwok, who was overseeing a major project in Beijing. Miles was hard to figure out—he was enormously energetic and entrepreneurial and clearly had very good connections. He flew us to Beijing and picked us up at the airport in his stretch Rolls-Royce, which was very unusual in that city. He showed us Morgan Plaza, the project he was building adjacent to the Olympic Village—a one-million-square-foot complex with three office and residential towers, including a 500,000-square-foot shopping center. He had also built offices across the street, but construction of the complex had stopped. We went to a dinner at his home. I've never seen a house quite like this in China—or elsewhere.

It is in the area where the top Chinese officials live in Beijing, adjacent to a lake, and his house had once been a rest home owned by the army for retired Chinese generals. It had a glass roof that could be walked on and was filled with incredible antiques. We had dinner in a living room more than fifty feet long, with the most luxurious furnishings. Miles very proudly took us on tour. He showed us the lower level where he had an Olympic-size swimming pool, a sauna, a steam room, and two beautiful antique Chinese scrolls hanging on the wall. When Phyllis admired them, he had an assistant take one down.

"These match the pair that was just donated to the Metropolitan Museum of Art by [New York financier and philanthropist] Oscar Tang, valued at $20 million each," Kwok said. Then he showed us a bedroom that had ten cots lined up.

"Who are those for?" I asked.

"For my security," he answered, which made us wonder what we were getting into.

"I've never seen a home any place like this," I said. "I think *Architectural Digest* would be fascinated. I know Paige Rense, the editor in chief."

The Pudong district skyline in Shanghai, China, along the Huangpu River.

"That's a good idea, Marvin," said Kwok.

"Can you arrange pictures?" I asked, and he agreed to do so. After all this, I was puzzled about why his construction project wasn't going forward. He said he was having problems with the authorities, whatever that meant. Clearly, he had a unique lifestyle.

We tried to raise $50 million for him. On his way to a meeting with us in New York, he stopped off in Beverly Hills, where he spent $100,000 on his wardrobe in order to be properly dressed, including a $40,000 suit that was decorated with gold thread. He gave me pictures of his house, but said, "I've thought about it. I think if *Architectural Digest* published this, I could get into trouble in China," which I thought was very sensible. We negotiated, but I became concerned about what was going on and I hired a very bright Chinese woman who had good connections to find out what she could about him. It turned out that he came from one of the provinces, had borrowed a good deal of money for his first development, and it was not clear if it had been repaid. It was believed that he was supported by the army, but there were other factions that were involved. Kwok is a very well-known name belonging to one of China's wealthiest families—though it wasn't Miles' birth name. We didn't hear from him for months. Then we got a letter from his assistant saying that he was in the hospital. We dropped the project, but in early in 2007, I got a call.

"Marvin, I'm going to be in New York at the Four Seasons Hotel. Can you come have tea with me?" I agreed to meet him. "I just want you to know that I'm finishing the project with the Beijing state authorities—they have supported me." He presented a book with all the letters of authorization to show me. He wanted me to see that he was legitimate. China is all about connections, and I suspect he liked taking the former chairman of Bloomingdale's and a former Miss America to meet people. I still do not know the whole story on Miles Kwok, but Morgan Plaza was completed and is today the most expensive project in Beijing with an average price of $7,064 per square meter. Half of the 192 apartments have been reserved, and there is a long waiting list for future residences. Word has it Bill Gates has rented a large space on the top floor.

(From top left) Miles Kwok, Phyllis George and her son Lincoln Brown, Lisa Block, and Marvin Traub. We are walking on his glass tiled roof in Beijing.

INDIA

Lee and I have been passionate about India since 1965. I was introduced to India by the textile designer Boris Kroll, the longtime president of Boris Kroll Fabrics, and fashion designer Adele Simpson. Bloomingdale's was the first store to actively import products from India.

Over the years, I've developed very close ties with the American ambassadors to India, whom I stayed with many times, including Chester Bowles, Kenneth Keating, John Gunther Dean (a Harvard College classmate), Robert Goheen and Richard Celeste. I knew people in the Indian government from Indira Gandhi to former Prime Minister Inder Gujral. We've traveled the country, as have our children. I have known India in the sixties, seventies, and eighties, when it was very difficult to do business there. In 2001, I was the keynote speaker at an All-Asia conference on retailing in New Delhi. I could see India was beginning to change. It had built its first three shopping centers, which I would then characterize as bad, worse, and awful. However, today, there are many new centers under construction.

I had known Mohan Murjani for a number of years. He was the original backer of Tommy Hilfiger. Mohan talked to me about the changes happening in India, and we formed a partnership. His son, Vijay, moved to Mumbai and set up an office there. They opened Tommy Hilfiger shops in India, and I introduced him to Robert Polet, the president, chairman and C.E.O. of the Gucci Group, Yves Carcelle, the chairman and C.E.O. of Louis Vuitton, as well as Maxine Clark, the C.E.O. of Build-a-Bear, Tom Murry, president of Calvin Klein, and Robert Bensoussan, then C.E.O. of Jimmy Choo.

Each time I went back to India, I became more concerned about Mohan's approach—each Hilfiger shop had a different local sponsor. We disagreed on this and dissolved our partnership after six months. Today Mohan has gone ahead with the lines I introduced him to, including Gucci and Jimmy Choo, Build-a-Bear and Calvin.

It became clear that India is a country undergoing enormous change. The

Lee loves India, Indian foods and cooking. Here she is wearing a sari with her good friend Usha Varadarajan, who manufactured designer bedspreads for Bloomingdale's, Ralph Lauren, and other fine stores.

economy is vibrant, and gross domestic product grows almost 9 percent annually. The combination of the growth of global telecommunications and the development of outsourcing is creating jobs for the young population. Half of India is below age twenty-five, and this is creating enormous economic opportunity and an emerging middle class seeking global brands.

Some experts believe that by 2050, India will unseat the United States as the planet's second-largest economy. Even today, India is the world's second-largest retail market, with most of the business being done in Mumbai or New Delhi. Indians, like the Chinese and the Japanese, have a thirst to purchase branded consumer goods. In the next decade, India will become one of the most important markets in the world.

Initially, we worked with Kishore Biyani, the managing director of Pantaloon Retail (India) and C.E.O. of the Future Group, who is the consummate Indian entrepreneur. Kishore is brash, outspoken, very creative, and has a unique, hard-driving personality. His concept, Big Bazaar, is a Wal-Mart–type store. His new 60,000-to-100,000-square foot stores are designed to look old and to create the perception of bargains by piling goods around the floor. Kishore sells rice out of bags. He organizes sales where he advertises, "Bring your old newspapers, and we'll buy them from you for [x] number of rupees a pound." It's a people's store. Indians relate to it, and it is very successful. His second chain, Pantaloons, is a specialty store selling moderately priced apparel. His third concept, Central, encompasses several 150,000-to-200,000-square-foot department stores, mostly leased with cosmetics, jeans, apparel, and accessories.

He was anxious to work with me, so I met him at his office in Mumbai.

"Marvin, I want to show you something," he said and took me out into the hall. There, blown up, larger than life, were my nineteen principles of retailing, as outlined in my first book. He had taken two pages from *Like No Other Store* and enlarged them so that everyone in his company could see them, learn them, and understand them.

Kishore and I worked together for a considerable period of time, but as I've discovered in India, when it comes time to renew a contract, it is common practice to renegotiate down, which I don't do. However, although our business relationship ended, we remain friends and mutual admirers.

Still, when Bob Fisher, the C.E.O. of the Gap, was recently in India, he met with Kishore, who said, "I work with Marvin Traub." (Later, he met with the Rahejas, another ex-client, and they said, "I work with Marvin Traub." And when he met with the Reliance Industries people, they said, "I work with Marvin Traub." I was working with none of them at that time, but they all claimed to be working with me.)

I moved on to work with Kishore's major competitor, Shopper's Stop, which is directed by B. S. Nagesh and owned by the K. Raheja Corporation, a family of major real estate developers from Mumbai. They built several 50,000-to-120,000 square-foot department stores that look much like a May company store did some ten or fifteen years ago. For India, this was a big step forward.

The Rahejas acquired huge amounts of property throughout India. The reason that India's initial shopping centers were so bad is that they were built by developers who then sold them off in pieces. One shopping center could have several different owners. The Rahejas learned from this and began to build better-quality shopping centers—not to American standards, but enormously better than the original Indian standards.

The Rahejas had the good sense to recognize that a shopping center in India could be more than a collection of stores. Now they are building centers tied in with apartments, office buildings, and technology centers. They call these new developments MindSpace.

Shopper's Stop was seeking to bring in new brands, which we helped with. We brought in Izod and developed a project with Target. However, I was frustrated that it was not doing more at the luxury level. I saw a big opportunity for companies like Ralph Lauren and Coach.

I was approached by a company called Reliance Industries, which is India's largest private-sector enterprise. Reliance set a goal to create the largest retail chain

in India. It projected that Indian retail business in 2010 would be about $300 billion. Reliance wanted 10 percent of that pie, or $30 billion. In order to do this, Reliance thought it needed two thousand stores. It wanted to create stores in the Wal-Mart image, selling goods at popular prices and food at very low prices. It set about recruiting an organization, organized the company into sixteen divisions, spent a great deal of money attracting C.E.O.'s, and spent months flying me back and forth for negotiations.

In August of 2006, while I was visiting Mumbai with Steve Waters of Compass Advisers, I met with Ratan Tata, whom I had known for many years. He is the chairman of Tata Sons, which controls the Tata Group, one of India's largest conglomerates, and is very charismatic. His uncle, J. R. D. Tata, was chairman of the Tata Group and in 1932 founded the airline now known as Air India.

Thirty years ago, Lee and I were very friendly with J. R. D. and his brother, Naval. Naval's wife, Simone, created a cosmetic company called Lakmé, which today is the major cosmetics brand in India. Naval and Simone had a beautiful home in India filled with European antiques, and they owned a home in Paris. They had two

(From left) Big Bazaar stores do 50 percent of their business in food—here selling rice from barrels; Marvin with Kishore Biyani, who changed retailing in India; the Taj Mahal Palace and Tower in Mumbai, owned by the Tata Group.

children, Ratan and Noel. Today, Noel is managing director of the Tata Group retail subsidiary Trent, and Ratan is the chairman of Tata Sons.

When I met with Ratan in August 2006, he told me that he was fascinated with Polo Ralph Lauren and upscale retail. He had lived in the United States for twelve years attending Riverdale Country School and Cornell University, where he studied architecture, and always enjoyed shopping at Polo stores.

"Marvin, I would like to bring Ralph Lauren to India," he said.

"That's a luxury brand, and I know the Polo Ralph Lauren team is looking for the right partners," I counseled. "Tata could represent them, but your retail concept today is not luxury."

Ratan suggested I meet with Raymond Bickson, a wonderful hotelier who is managing director of Taj Hotels. We met at the Pierre Hotel, which was acquired by Taj Hotels in September 2006. Taj also acquired the Ritz-Carlton in Boston.

We ended up being retained by Tata for the hotel group and separately by Noel, who wanted to import brands like the Gap. We've been working together since early 2007. We believe the two brands we are working on, Ralph Lauren and Coach, would be a great success. Meanwhile, Noel has become more interested in the opportunities for upscale retailing.

I set up a meeting for Ratan with Ralph and Roger Farah to review the possible project. It went well. Two weeks later, Ralph and his wife, Ricky, invited Ratan, Lee, and me to dinner at their home in Bedford. Ralph and Ratan share a common passion for cars. After dinner, Ralph showed us twelve extraordinary cars from his collection, including his wonderful McLaren, which has the driver's seat in the middle. Meanwhile, Ratan discussed his new custom-made Maserati, as well as his automobile company, Tata Motors, which will produce the Nano, the first inexpensive car for India at $2,500. It is a project that will revolutionize the automobile industry in that country. Clearly, the two industry leaders bonded, and our discussions were off to a good start. After two years, we are still reviewing—but we are hopeful. It could be a major commitment for each side, but if it happens it will take time.

We also worked with another group, DLF, a leading real estate developer in India, which was headed by chairman K. P. Singh. We advised Pia Singh, his daughter, who is in charge of developing the first luxury shopping center for India, opening spring 2008.

Today, most major consumer companies want to come to India. In Dubai and in Moscow, there are relatively low duty rates and it's easy to do business. In India, the duties are among the highest in the world, plus there are additional taxes. There are also regulations that off-shore firms cannot own more than 51 percent of a company and therefore need local partners. Today, the brands that are sold in India are all struggling to make money within this structure.

Most of the luxury shops in India are in hotels, such as the Taj Mahal Palace in Mumbai, part of the Tata Group, because the shopping centers are much too downscale. There is no Madison Avenue, Bond Street, or rue de Faubourg Saint-Honoré in India. But there are three hundred shopping centers being planned. The world's major retail players are all trying to enter the country and are attempting to find the right partners, which is creating an enormous amount of real estate activity.

The Indian stock market is booming. Both Shopper's Stop and the Future Group—Kishore Biyani's company—sell at extraordinary multiples. Clearly, India will be a very different place in ten years. According to *Forbes* in 2008, four of the eight wealthiest men in the world are Indian billionaires.

GREECE AND ROMANIA

I started working in Athens in 2005 with a very outgoing and ebullient Greek businessman named Constantin Lambropoulos. Constantin is from an old Greek family that had operated a 90,000-square-foot store called Lambropoulos, which they built with another group. They sold it and were building a 250,000-square-foot store called Attica. We were hired to help plan it.

The new store was adjacent to the best hotel in Athens, the Grand Bretagne. We helped them add brands, including Elie Tahari, Juicy Couture, Stuart Weitzman, and a number of others. We worked aggressively with Estée Lauder to plan the cosmetics department, and today Attica is the best Jo Malone account in Europe.

There is also a new shopping center being planned for Athens adjacent to the former Olympic Village—a 600,000-square-foot structure in the middle of a very wealthy suburb of the city. Constantin wanted to do an upscale 120,000-square-foot department store. He and his general merchandise manager flew to Dubai where they toured Harvey Nichols Dubai; met our chief merchant, Eda

Kuloglu; and toured the Saks Fifth Avenue store as well. Afterward, we talked.

"We like the look of Harvey Nichols," Constantin said, "and we would like you to help plan and merchandise our new store."

As we worked with Constantin, we got to know his associate Alessandro Stocco, who worked with Elmec, a separate division that operates in Eastern Europe. In January, Alessandro visited New York to discuss the emerging market of Bucharest, Romania, a city of increasing affluence and a growing taste for luxury, particularly since Romania joined the common market. Elmec operates a number of successful multibrand stores in Bucharest, featuring such brands as Polo Ralph Lauren, Levi Strauss, and Burberry that were doing very well. It was developing two parcels in the city that would support 100,000-square-foot stores—one in an emerging upscale mall; the other in a beautiful, historic building.

We all agreed it could be a great opportunity for a Saks Fifth Avenue store. And at this early stage, Morty Singer met with Alessandro and David Pilnick, in charge of international expansion for Saks Fifth Avenue, to develop a

A glorious view of Athens, Greece.

strategy for Saks Bucharest. All are optimistic about this city's potential for Saks and key luxury brands. We believe Romania today is a similar opportunity to Moscow in 1993.

KOREA

In 1985, I retained a very bright Korean woman, Sung-Joo Kim, to help with the planning of a Bloomingdale's country promotion of Korea. Sung-Joo was the daughter of one of the leading industrialists of South Korea. Though she was educated at Amherst, the London School of Economics, and Harvard, her father would not permit her to participate in the family business. So Sung-Joo introduced Gucci to South Korea—becoming the fifth-largest Gucci franchise in the world. Sung-Joo's group also set up Yves Saint Laurent, Sonia Rykiel, and Marks & Spencer exclusively for Korea.

When I first spoke about the Bloomingdale's promotion, the Koreans were enthusiastic and charming, but when I arrived in Seoul, they turned out to be very demanding. This was the first and only country promotion that I canceled. What remained was my friendship with Sung-Joo, and in 2005, we found occasion to work together again.

In the 1980s, MCM, which stood for Michael Cromer München, was a major luxury brand. MCM had a boutique on Fifty-seventh Street in New York. The bags sold well at Bloomingdale's and other fine stores. It was a $500 million business. Then Michael Cromer got into trouble with the tax authorities in Germany and the business disappeared—except for South Korea and Japan.

In South Korea, Sung-Joo had the license and operated some seventy shops doing more than $80 million annually. This became the bulk of the MCM business worldwide. Sung-Joo quickly decided it was better to own the company than pay royalties, so she acquired it. She hired our team to consult on rebuilding the brand and rebuilding distribution in the United States. Today, MCM is growing globally with freestanding stores in Beijing, on Sloane Street in London, and in Munich.

There are also plans for the United States. Brand recognition is increasing, and volume has doubled.

We brought in Robert Burke, the former men's fashion director at Bergdorf Goodman, to help style the line for the United States. MCM was relaunched at Colette in Paris, an event at Corso Como in Milan, and in many other fine stores throughout Europe. In America, it was relaunched at Bloomingdale's Fifty-ninth Street and at eight other of Bloomingdale's most important stores in September 2007.

I had the privilege of presenting an award to Sung-Joo when she was honored at the Spirit of Asian America Gala in 2007, sponsored by the Asian American Federation of New York. She was also selected by the *Wall Street Journal* as one of the top fifty women to watch in the world and has been recognized by *Forbes*, CNN, CNBC, and the World Economic Forum in Davos. She's very dedicated to the power of women in business.

Sung-Joo and me in my new office looking at a hot new color in MCM. She's a powerhouse yet fun to work with.

I met Marvin Traub shortly after joining Bloomingdale's as a merchant trainee in 1986. Marvin always took a keen interest in the young executives. He interacted with us, listened to us and nurtured us. When I decided to apply to Harvard Business School, Marvin could not have been more helpful or supportive.
Jim Gold, Chairman and C.E.O. of Bergdorf Goodman

It would be totally inappropriate to use the past tense when evaluating Marvin Traub's influence on my career. I was a rookie salesman at the Manhattan Shirt Company when I first met him and then had the wonderful and challenging experience of interfacing with Marvin throughout our careers until I became the chief executive officer of my company, and then after that an investment manager in the financial community. All this time, and still today, I have been learning from Marvin. The glass is half full; one can start with adversity and manipulate it until it becomes success. Marvin taught me by example the lesson of leadership with enthusiasm, while earning the devotion and loyalty of those who worked for him. All this time, he demonstrated the highest level of creativity, featuring a magnificently inquisitive mind-set that I have always tried to emulate.
Larry Leeds, chairman of Buckingham Capital Management

ELIE TAHARI

Elie Tahari is unique in our industry. He arrived in the United States from Israel in the 1970s with no job but found work as an electrician in the garment district. After observing what people did there, he believed that he could do it better and became a designer.

Bloomingdale's was fortunate to partner with Elie in the 1980s. He was talented, outspoken, and not always easy to work with, but we built a great business together. Over time, Elie Tahari became the leading bridge supplier of Saks Fifth Avenue, Bloomingdale's, and Bergdorf Goodman, as well as a major supplier of Neiman Marcus. Elie was a great success, but his business was mainly in the United States. In spring 2005, I invited him to lunch to talk about the growing opportunities for international growth, and he retained Marvin Traub Associates.

After working with our friends in Dubai, Moscow, London, Paris, and Hong Kong, the Elie Tahari international business exceeded $5 million in retail within a year. Elie Tahari was the number-one apparel brand at TsUM in Moscow and Harvey Nichols Dubai. Not surprisingly, Elie is happy, and I feel a real affirmation of our belief in international expansion. The potential remains for building a very substantial global business.

Elie Tahari's family—daughter Zoe, son Jeremey, and wife Rory, who is hugely influential in his business today.

LENNY KRAVITZ

Not all of our projects are overseas. In 2005, Claude Arpels, who headed the U.S. operations of Van Cleef and Arpels, introduced us to Lenny Kravitz, a most unusual and successful musician and singer who aspired in his second career to become the next Ralph Lauren or Calvin Klein. He was probably driven to succeed by his parents—his mother was the late, beautiful actress Roxie Roker, and his father, Sy Kravitz, was a filmmaker and television news producer at NBC who initially bankrolled his son's music career.

I invited Carl Levine, the former senior vice president for home furnishings at Bloomingdale's, and Dawn Mello, the former president of Bergdorf Goodman, to join our team. We visited Lenny at his waterfront home in Miami. Lenny had a closet in his house with jackets and trousers custom made for him by Gucci, Giorgio Armani, and Roberto Cavalli, as well as a collection of vintage women's clothing for singers who performed with him. He had custom-made contemporary clothing and furniture his team created as well. This would be the beginnings of his collection.

We introduced him to Elie Tahari and spent a year trying to create the House of Lenny Kravitz. At the end of the year, we could not reach closure on funding, so we dropped the project but remained friends.

I got a good many brownie points from my grandchildren, particularly when Lee and I took them to a Lenny Kravitz concert at the Beacon Theatre in New York. I quickly understood why Lenny had suggested we might want earplugs and warned us we would have to stand for two hours, which we did. I was impressed—the Lenny Kravitz on the stage was very different from the Lenny Kravitz who was trying to create a contemporary apparel collection. And when Lenny and his teenage daughter joined us at the Rainbow Room to help celebrate my eightieth birthday, my young friends thought we were pretty cool.

Me, Lenny Kravitz, and my grandson, Alexander.

DONALD TRUMP

I've known Donald Trump for more than twenty years. When Bloomingdale's was for sale in 1989, I received a call from him.

"I'd like to be your partner in buying Bloomingdale's," Donald said. "We don't have to change the name to Trump, but we should consider calling it 'Trump's Bloomingdale's.'"

I passed, as I was working with Thomas Lee. Nevertheless, Donald Trump is an extraordinary brand. One of our clients is Drinks Americas, a publicly listed company in the liquor and beverage field. I was one of the first investors. C.E.O. Patrick Kenny, who started the company, came from Seagram's. He knew the industry and had worked with me at Sweet16.com, an ill-fated Web site targeted to teenagers that counted Britney Spears as its major asset. Despite her involvement, it blew up when the dot-com bubble burst.

Drinks Americas produced Old Whiskey River, Willie Nelson's bourbon, Roy Yamaguchi's sake, and Paul Newman's carbonated drinks, Newman's Own Lightly Sparkling Fruit Juices. Patrick believed vodka would be a great addition, and we decided that Donald Trump would be a great brand. I approached Donald, and he was interested. Our final meeting in his office involved three television crews. Donald promised to "negotiate the shit out of us," which he did, but we made a deal, a snippet of which was shown on *The Apprentice*. We announced Trump: The World's Finest Super Premium Vodka in November 2005 before a packed house at Trump Tower in Manhattan, complete with dancing girls, music, and great press. Donald's goal is to exceed Grey Goose, and after one year, his vodka is ahead of Grey Goose's pace, despite the fact that The Donald does not drink.

Morty Singer developed another exciting project with Donald's children Ivanka and Donald, Jr. The Trump Ocean Club International Hotel and Tower will be the largest mixed-use real estate project in Panama when it opens in 2010. Since it was renamed and remarketed, the developers have been able to command prices that are 40 to 50 percent higher and the structure has grown an impressive twelve floors to sixty-six floors—the

largest building in Panama and highly lucrative for Donald. I enjoy working with Donald. He is colorful, imaginative, and outspoken—with an enormous ego—but underneath all that, he is very creative, a smart businessman, a tough negotiator, and a dedicated father.

HALSTON AND BILL BLASS

In the spring of 2007, I received a visit from John Semel, a bright young Wall Streeter who is the senior vice president of business development at the Weinstein Company, run by Harvey and Bob Weinstein. In addition to producing movies, Harvey has a passion for fashion. His wife, Georgina Chapman, cofounded and codesigns Marchesa, a successful designer brand. He is a coproducer of the wildly successful Bravo reality TV show *Project Runway* and was interested in finding a partner to acquire the Halston brand and develop it with him.

(Left) Donald Trump holding a bottle of The World's Finest Super Premium Vodka.
(Right) A rendering of the Trump Ocean Club International Hotel and Tower.

Harvey had a great strategy: He could make a movie about Halston and suggest that the stars who work with him wear Halston on the red carpet (I gather that in Hollywood, stars take his suggestions very seriously), and he could also promote Halston on *Project Runway*.

I had known Halston well. Bloomingdale's sold his collection, but more important, he was dedicated to dance, in particular to the Martha Graham Dance Company and to Martha herself. He designed costumes, contributed money, and spent time with the company. My wife, Lee, who studied with Martha when she was in high school, was not only the former chairperson, and now chair emerita of the dance company's board of trustees but had been a close personal friend of and adviser to Martha. One of the great privileges and joys of our life was sitting backstage with Martha, watching the company perform.

Halston was a product of the 1970s and all that went with it—Andy Warhol, Studio 54, a wild lifestyle, recreational drugs, and all-night parties. Despite having great talent (he started as a milliner at Bergdorf Goodman), he hurt his image by selling his name and making inexpensive Halston clothes for J. C. Penney. By the time of his death in 1990, the business had gone downhill.

A number of recent attempts to revive his collection had failed, but I thought Harvey had a good idea. I called Jamie Salter, an aggressive, outspoken Canadian apparelmaker who is the C.E.O. of Hilco Consumer Capital, owned by Hilco Trading, with Jeffrey Hecktman. I knew they were seeking brands, as they had just tried to purchase Adrienne Vittadini. They were interested, so I set up a lunch with Jamie, Jeffrey, Harvey, John Semel, Aslaug, Morty, and me. It was in Harvey's office, catered by Robert De Niro's restaurant, Tribeca Grill, since Harvey and the actor are partners.

Harvey is a dominating, shrewd, aggressive dealmaker, but so are Jamie and Jeffrey. The lunch was conducted in larger-than-life decibels, but by the time the dessert was served, a partnership was beginning. The Weinsteins, with Jamie and Jeffrey, acquired Halston and raised $25 million. I received a success fee, and I look forward to the Halston collection and the movie. Who will play Halston and Martha?

In the same time period, I was being recruited by Robert D'Loren, president and C.E.O. of NexCen Brands, to join the board of his company. NexCen is about building and licensing brands and has acquired several, including Waverly Fabrics, Athlete's Foot, and Bill Blass. It's mission is to develop strategies for each of these brands and license them out with support and strategy coming from the corporate parent. Bob was particularly anxious for me to be involved with the international aspects of the companies and to facilitate the development of Bill Blass, which has great potential.

Bill Blass had also been a good friend of mine. My mother, Bea, a fashion director at Bonwit Teller, had been one of his early supporters. When she passed away, in 1981, Bill joined me in creating the Bea Traub Fashion Research Library at the Fashion Institute of Technology.

I am enthusiastic about NexCen because I believe Bob is a great talent. I share belief in the concept, but I also told him that at eighty-one, I was too old to join the board of a public company.

"It's your contribution and knowledge that are critical to us, not your age," Bob countered.

I met and liked my fellow directors-to-be and agreed to join the board. Two weeks later, *Women's Wear Daily* ran the story that one of NexCen's directors was retiring because of age—I believe he was seventy-five. Two weeks after that, *WWD* ran the story that I was joining the board but fortunately neglected to list my age. It will be interesting to see how these two brands, Halston and Bill Blass, which are competing for the same store open-to-buy but for different customers, will fare.

BLUE LAGOON

In the spring of 2007, Aslaug introduced me to two entrepreneurial fellow Icelanders, Grimur Saemundsen and Sigurdur Thorsteinsson. Grimur is a doctor and an athlete, the former captain of the Iceland National Football League, and a businessman. Siggi's background is in marketing and design, in both Iceland and Italy.

They had an unusual project. The major tourist attraction of Iceland is the Blue Lagoon—a unique warm-water natural geothermal spa that attracts 400,000 visitors annually to a country of 300,000. The lagoon is considered the Eiffel Tower of Iceland. The Blue Lagoon is the result of a volcanic eruption thousands of years ago, and the water contains algae and silicone that are beneficial for the skin. People with skin diseases such as psoriasis come from all over the world to bathe in the Blue Lagoon.

Grimur had set up a company that owns the Blue Lagoon and with dermatologists developed a Blue Lagoon skin-care collection. It was being marketed successfully in Scandinavia, Germany, and in three shops in Iceland. They wondered if Marvin Traub Associates could develop and implement a distribution and spa strategy for the United States and other international locations. It was an interesting assignment. The product was very credible and had substantial merchant support. It helped that ever since Aslaug joined our team, I've been intrigued by Iceland. In June, Lee, Aslaug, and I flew to Reykjavik for an Icelandic weekend. Iceland turned out to be a fascinating green country with attractive, friendly people. Legend has it that Iceland was settled by Vikings from Scandinavia in the ninth century who stopped in Ireland on their way to Norway to pick up a group of beautiful Celtic women who are said to be the ancestors of today's Icelanders. We traveled to the Blue Lagoon, and it was unique. It is about thirty miles from Reykjavik, in Grindavik, and set in a field that looks like a lunar landscape.

We had lunch, saw the lagoon, and toured the company's research and production facilities. The next day, Lee and I returned for massages in the warm lagoon water. One lies on a rubber mattress and the masseur stands in the water. It is pleasant and very refreshing. Afterward, they wrap you in a white robe and you feel very good.

The Blue Lagoon, in Iceland.

That evening, we had a wonderful dinner at the Lava Restaurant there and stayed overnight at the clinic where people come from all over the world for treatment. The next morning, we bathed in the Blue Lagoon pool at the clinic; after our second bath we were totally sold on the product. We met with Siggi and Grimur and were retained to develop and implement distribution strategies for the skin-care products and spas.

Subsequently we met with four New York retailers and agreed on an exclusive spring 2008 launch in eight Saks Fifth Avenue stores, including New York and Beverly Hills. Saks tested the product and thought it was great. Saks actually photographed a 2006 catalog at the Blue Lagoon and was very enthusiastic about the Icelandic image of water, nature, and purity. We are developing a separate spa strategy, and, after the Saks launch, expect to role out the Blue Lagoon product internationally. We are building the organization and have already hired Suzanne Fedorczyk from Shiseido to be the sales manager.

The Blue Lagoon shop in Iceland. Blue Lagoon skin-care products are made from mud from the Blue Lagoon.

KIRA PLASTININA

In the spring of 2007, Morty received a call from Pierre Mallevays, a former LVMH executive who is a friend and founder and managing partner at luxury-goods consultancy Savigny Partners. Pierre suggested that we meet Sergei Plastinin, a Russian entrepreneur who he felt could use our help. Sergei came to New York and met with Morty.

"You have to hear this story," Morty told me.

In 1991, after perestroika, there were great opportunities for entrepreneurially-minded Russians. Sergei Plastinin seized the moment and developed the first baby food and yogurt business in Russia, Wimm-Bill-Dann Foods. Sergei partnered with various suppliers and took the company public on the American stock exchange. Today, WBD has a market capitalization of more than $5 billion. With that affluence behind him, Sergei could follow up with his great passion—his talented, then fourteen-year-old daughter Kira, who loves fashion. Sergei was an unusual Russian businessman—sound and low-key yet thoughtful and creative.

He set up a company to implement Kira's design ideas and sketches, had the clothes made in China, and in six months opened eighteen stores in Russia—nine in Moscow and nine throughout the country. The project got enormous publicity. Kira became the best-known teenager in the country, and according to Sergei, the eighteen stores will do between $25 million and $30 million in their first year. He visited us because he wanted to open fifty stores in the United States in 2008. By then, Kira would be fifteen. I gently suggested we could start with ten or twelve stores, but thought I needed to visit Russia before I became involved.

I was planning to visit Moscow in May 2007 for the opening of Polo Ralph Lauren, so I tied the two events together. I visited two Moscow shopping centers and was pleasantly surprised with what I found—stores in the image of a Russian H&M doing business with healthy traffic and smiling young customers.

We decided this was a case where our partnership with SD Retail Consulting would be helpful, because it could plan the back of the house. Morty Singer and David Ressinger of SD flew to Moscow. We were retained by Sergei and started down an extraordinary new route. Sergei has been very supportive. We hired one of the best search firms, Herbert Mines Associates, to recruit top talent; Laura Pomerantz of PBS Real Estate, one of the best real estate firms, to find locations; one of the best public relations firms, Harrison & Shriftman, to handle publicity; and one of the top designers, Kenneth Nisch, chairman of JGA, to design the stores. In short order, we were putting together a major retail chain. We have leases for five stores in the New York City region and six stores in Los Angeles, all eleven opening between May and August of 2008. Sergei plans to have his corporate offices in Los Angeles and build a second home in Beverly Hills.

Kira is a surprisingly modest, soft-spoken young lady who speaks fluent English and is a good student. She attends school from 8 a.m. to 3:30 p.m., and on Tuesdays, Thursdays, and sometimes Saturdays, she goes to the office and works on her collection. She also studies the piano, and on Fridays, rides horses and practices dressage. She is looking forward to moving to California. We expect to build a fifty to one-hundred or more store chain, unlike anything in the United States, around the talents of a fifteen-year-old young lady—this has to be one of the more unusual projects that we have ever undertaken. Morty is intrigued and is spending a great deal of time on it. I find myself spending time as well, because it is such a demanding project. After an appropriate introduction by Harrison & Shriftman, our PR firm, Dylan Lauren, Ralph's daughter, was intrigued by Kira and the project; so each store will feature a Dylan's Candy Bar— an exciting addition.

In early January, Harrison & Shriftman set up a reception for Kira to meet the press in a downtown exhibit space. It went very well; Kira proved herself to be an unusually poised fifteen-year-old who charmed the press and handled the TV cameras with ease. The teenage models looked very good in her spring collection. It is an exciting beginning for a unique retailing saga.

Kira Plastinina is a one-of-a-kind designer. She started sketching at age seven and now, at age fifteen, designs for her own multinational chain of stores.

ELLEN TRACY

When I was C.E.O. of Bloomingdale's, the leading supplier of bridge apparel was Ellen Tracy, which was started as a blouse company in 1949 by a crusty, much-beloved and respected businessman named Herb Gallen. Herb enjoyed running the a very profitable company that did 60 percent of its business with Saks, Bloomingdale's, and Neiman Marcus and afforded him a corporate jet and a 200-foot yacht.

Nevertheless, when Herb was eighty-two, Gilbert Harrison and I persuaded him to consider selling the business to Bain Capital. At the last minute, Herb backed out. He didn't want a boss and was having too much fun. Two years later we were back. Herb was eighty-four and agreed to a carefully orchestrated sale—he did not want an auction.

We sold it to Liz Claiborne for $180 million (approximate annual Ellen Tracy volume) and Herb and his wife, creative director and guiding spirit Linda Allard, agreed to stay on. Linda not only supervised design, she was the customer and made Ellen Tracy special. Unfortunately, it did not work out; Herb and Linda were uncomfortable having a boss. It was a different and difficult environment for both of them and they left in less than six months.

Immediately, the business declined and with a series of management changes, new designers and changes at the parent Liz Claiborne by 2007, volume was down over 50 percent and profits showed a similar decline.

By summer 2007, Bill McComb, the new C.E.O. of Liz Claiborne, was anxious to restructure the company and put eight of the major brands up for sale (after having sold off or closed some smaller brands). Ellen Tracy was among them.

I knew and understood the brand so I was able to join Bill Sweedler and his team. He was an entrepreneur as well as an apparel manufacturer. I knew Bill and had worked with his father at Ralph Lauren. Other principals—Stuart Jamison, a venture capitalist neighbor and friend of Bill's, and Barry Sternlicht, former principal of Starwood—joined Bill in acquiring Ellen Tracy. Subsequently, Jamie Salter and Jeffery Hecktman of Hilco joined them to create a larger platform. I joined during the due diligence period,

Traub, Partners Buy Ellen Tracy for $42.3M

About five years after Marvin Traub helped sell Ellen Tracy to Liz Claiborne Inc., Traub and his new business partners are hoping to fulfill the vision Claiborne had for the bridge brand at the time but never achieved.

Radius Partners LLC, Windsong Brands LLC, Barry Sternlicht and Traub bought Ellen Tracy for $42.3 million — a substantial discount from the reported $180 million Claiborne spent to acquire the bridge label from Herbert Gallen and Linda Allard. Together the buyers are setting up two companies, a holding side that will own the label and an operating side to produce the sportswear, creating a platform from which they can acquire other women's apparel businesses.

"We wouldn't be doing this if we didn't think we could get it back to its heyday," Traub said. "When I was at Bloomingdale's, Ellen Tracy was our leading supplier in bridge, and when the brand was originally sold to Liz, they said they wanted to take it to a much higher level. We can take it to that higher level."

Of course, the 59-year-old brand is worse for wear since Claiborne bought it. Ellen Tracy did about $171 million in volume at the time and was the leading

A spring Ellen Tracy look.

at Claiborne, sources said.

The expansion, including a New York flagship, likely will coincide with spring 2009, the first season under the new owners, after they feel the product is where it should be.

Cleaning up the back office also will be a priority.

Sternlicht said they have the sourcing capabilities established. He and William Sweedler — chief executive officer of Windsong Brands LLC — have teamed up before, investing in moderate brand Caribbean Joe and denim resource Joe's Jeans.

The consortium had been negotiating the deal for the last four months, after originally bidding on five of the brands, including Dana Buchman, Laundry, Prana and C&C California. "Originally we'd looked at all the brands, and we'd seen Ellen Tracy as the crown jewel," said Sweedler. "With Dana Buchman, we were not sure we wanted to be competing with two brands in the same space, though."

Claiborne decided last month to license Dana Buchman to Kohl's, where it will become a moderate resource, and they predict that Ellen Tracy will benefit from eliminating the competition of a fellow traditional bridge brand.

"We wouldn't be doing this if we didn't think we could get it back to its heyday.... We can take it to that higher level. "

— Marvin Traub, Marvin Traub Associates Inc.

resource in the booming bridge department. The slide to about $100 million today was propelled by the weakening of the traditional bridge market, product problems and recent economic woes.

The new buyers have several plans for the brand: adding Ellen Tracy full-priced retail stores, expanding internationally and launching a national marketing campaign. First, though, they must hire a designer, after George Sharp resigned last month to join St. John as executive vice president of design, as well as a business head. They said they are already in talks with several candidates. They plan to keep on "the lion's share" of the 77 core brand employees and 100-plus retail outlet employees. Ellen Tracy interim president Ann Bukawyn, a licensing veteran who has been at Claiborne since the Nineties and was installed as interim president in June during the vendor's restructuring, likely will take a new role

After four long months of negotiations, they also got a deal, according to analysts. Claiborne sold substantially all of Ellen Tracy's assets and liabilities for a $27.3 million cash payment, subject to inventory adjustment payable at closing, and a contingent cash payment of up to $15 million based on brand performance through 2012, while Claiborne will retain approximately $8.2 million in net working capital, excluding inventory.

"Most of [Claiborne's] deals have been for inventory value," said Brad Stephens, a retail analyst for Morgan Keegan & Co. Inc. "They've been giving the brands away."

— W.B.

facilitated a meeting with the corporate management and we acquired the company for a $27.3 million cash payment plus a potential additional of $15 million based on performance. So less than five years after selling, I helped to buy it back. Quite a mark-down! And a wonderful opportunity. As I write this, we are finalizing our strategies and seeking proper management and design talent to restore the brand to its former eminent position. Saks, Neiman's, and Bloomingdale's are very supportive. There is enormous enthusiasm for the brand and high expectations.

Now on to turning around the business—a very exciting and difficult challenge. We recognize this, and look forward to it.

ANDRÉ 3000

While writing this book, I found that I was continuously approached by prospective new clients. However, I had decided that the last new client to include should be Kira. She was unique enough.

But then, in December 2007, I was approached by André Benjamin. André, also known as André 3000, was one half of the hip-hop group Outkast and costar of Will Ferrell's *Semi-Pro,* which was the number-one movie at the box office in February 2008. André has his own unique style and has achieved enormous success selling records and in his movie appearances. Although I was not very familiar with him, his name provoked an extraordinary and very positive response from many people. Aslaug and I met with him.

André wanted to develop a menswear collection around a different theme each season, and he had done his homework. He had sought advice from Ralph Lauren, Anna Wintour, the editor in chief of *Vogue,* and Tom Ford. He retained a designer to work with him on the collection and an experienced executive to source it in Hong Kong and Milan. He produced a video to present the background for his first fall collection, based on American football circa 1900 to 1935. It was right-on and focused on major contemporary trends combining vintage with sport. Aslaug and I

The Benjamin Bixby collection received an extraordinary response from the press for a new line including the flip cover of the 2008 Spring Fashion issue of *New York Magazine* and a full page in *DNR,* the men's fashion trade publication.

NEW YORK

MEN'S FASHION

André 3000
(a.k.a. Benjamin)
is just dandy
pg. 224

PLUS
Kurt Andersen on **Your Political Destiny**

John Heilemann on **Hillary** and the Press

Ariel Levy on **k.d. lang,** America's Butch Sweetheart

(Flip magazine over for Spring Fashion, Women's Edition)

were impressed by him, by his degree of preparation, and by the fact that everywhere we went, people recognized him. Strangers greeted him, gave him high fives, and deluged him with comments like, "Man, you are terrific." He was gracious with each person.

We were immediately retained and spent the next few days beginning our work with André. This became a major project for Aslaug. We introduced him to Hamilton South, a top public relations firm, to a search firm, and we made a decision to show his first collection in the Gramercy Park Hotel in Manhattan one month later.

I recruited my good friend Stanley Tucker, the former senior vice president of Burberry Men's. Prior to that, Stan was fashion director of menswear, children's wear, and home furnishings at Saks Fifth Avenue and C.O.O. of Geoffrey Beene. We retained him to work with us on the launch of André's collection—his background is perfect for an upscale menswear collection with an updated traditional feel. We received an incredible international response to a new line—orders from Barneys, Bergdorf, Bloomingdale's, Neiman Marcus, Harrods, Harvey Nichols in London, Harvey Nichols Dubai, TsUM in Moscow, and United Arrows Japan. We have planned major launches in September 2008 with André at Barneys New York and Harrods London.

It's so interesting to look back over the past decade. I believed in globalization, and it became the basis of my business. Marvin Traub Associates is currently active in fourteen countries: Russia, India, China (including Hong Kong), Dubai, Greece, Turkey, Canada, Italy, France, the United Kingdom, Romania, Panama, and Iceland, as well as the United States. In 2007, I logged 210,000 air miles.

A NEW BUSINESS

Over the years, Morty Singer and I frequently thought about the possibility of raising a fund. In our consulting business, we saw many quality companies that needed an infusion of capital, but we were not in a position to meet those needs. When Aslaug Magnusdottir joined us in the fall of 2006, it seemed an appropriate time to take a fresh look. In her three years with Baugur, the Icelandic venture capital fund, Aslaug had overseen a dozen transactions of all sizes in the United Kingdom.

As we looked at the financial markets, we became aware that there are a great many funds anxious to invest $50 million to $100 million or more, but there was a large gap for midsized, healthy companies that needed to raise $5 million to $25 million. This is because large funds, with their overhead, prefer to invest $50 million or more in order to capitalize on their assets. I often make the point that if Ralph Lauren had been looking for money when he started his tie business decades ago, most of these investors would have passed on him because he was too small. So we selected the $5 million to $25 million niche. We formed a new company—TSM (for Traub, Singer, and Magnusdottir) Capital—in which we would all be equal partners and all be equally involved. It was my goal to build something for the future, for them as well as for me. We decided initially that we would invest on a deal-by-deal basis.

We announced the creation of the fund and the closing of our first deal simultaneously. It made the front page of *Women's Wear Daily* with the headline "Marvin's Bigger Room." I was flattered that *WWD* put "Marvin" in the headline, assuming its readers would immediately know which Marvin it was talking about. As soon as the story ran in *WWD*, our phones began ringing with people looking to invest or to attract investments.

The first company we chose was Matthew Williamson, a profitable, $20-million business. Matthew is the creative director of Emilio Pucci, as well as the designer of his own collection. He's very talented. Today, he has 170 accounts in 42 countries, but his business in America is relatively small. Prior to joining us, Auslaug worked with him and continues to do so.

I'm very impressed with Matthew because he is one of a limited number of designers who not only cares passionately about press and receptivity but also about building a healthy, profitable business. That's a quality that one rarely sees. I felt that if we were going to work with a designer, it should be one with whom our interests are aligned.

We're taking on the responsibility of building a business for him in America by expanding his retail and wholesale business and developing a licensing strategy. In order to do this, we have brought in Jeffrey Aronsson, the former president and C.E.O. of Donna Karan and Oscar de la Renta. I will be on the Matthew Williamson board and will travel to London several times a year. Matthew did his tenth anniversary ready-to-wear show in that city, and the occasion was celebrated by the Design Museum in London. It did a retrospective in October 2007 based on his enormous reputation for use of color, prints, and fabrics.

At TSM Capital, we have specific criteria that make it easier to sort out the many proposals that we receive. We don't invest in start-ups, and we don't do turnarounds. We are interested in working only with companies where we can make a significant difference. And we invest in companies that are currently profitable or will be within twelve months. We also invest in firms with a global outlook and look forward to expanding our portfolio.

From a philosophical point of view, the idea of starting a new business at age eighty-two, one that adds more staff, more responsibilities, and more office space, is somewhat off-the-charts. There are some people, such as myself, who think it's wonderful and that I'm fortunate and blessed to be able to do it. Every day, I look forward to making all this happen. This is really about building for the future for my team. I'm grateful to be working with such bright and talented young people. I'm enthusiastic and believe we can develop a substantial number of new projects in the coming years.

This August 28, 2007, *WWD* story announced the creation of TSM Capital and its first investment.

Women's Wear Daily • The Retailers' Daily Newspaper • August 28, 2007 • $2.00

WWD TUESDAY

Ready-to-Wear/Textiles

The Short Run

PYTs are in luck. The shortest of shorts are back with a vengeance in a bounty of chic variations. Here, M Missoni's cotton and spandex shorts, worn with a playful metallic cardigan and printed bra top; Alex Woo necklaces. For more, see pages 6 and 7.

Marvin's Bigger Room: New Traub-Led Group Invests in Williamson

By Marc Karimzadeh

NEW YORK — Marvin Traub is starting yet another chapter in his storied career.

The former chairman and chief executive officer of Bloomingdale's has partnered with Mortimer Singer and Aslaug Magnusdottir to create TSM Capital to invest in designer businesses, brands and retailers in the early stages of their companies, with revenues of between $5 million and $50 million.

And Traub and his partners have wasted no time in their goal to create a portfolio of up to 10 businesses over the next three years. The trio is launching TSM Capital by taking a stake in

See **Traub**, *Page* **10**

THE FUTURE OF RETAILING

I n 1993, I coined nineteen "Retailing Principles for the Nineties," for my first book, *Like No Other Store*, and in rereading them today, I've realized they seem as appropriate now as they were then. I wrote of the need for centralization, direct marketing, identifying global opportunities, approaching retailing as theater, and using various organizational principles. I feel these principles are still germane today. But before writing about the future of retailing from the perspective of 2008, it's worth noting the changes that have occurred in the fifteen years since I published my first book and where I think these changes are taking us.

In the realm of the American department store, the trend toward centralization has moved at breakneck speed. In 1993, there were about twenty-five major and minor department-store nameplates. In 2008, there are eleven. Of that number, there are only five major department-store players left; Dillard's, Nordstrom, Lord & Taylor, Belk, and Macy's. Upscale retailers include Neiman Marcus, Saks Fifth Avenue, Bloomingdale's, and Barneys New York. Moderate-priced retailers include Kohl's and J. C. Penney, plus the major discounters. Has this been good for consumers? Clearly, their choices are narrowing.

Americans have grown up with the image of the downtown department store as much more than a place to shop—these stores are a part of our childhood memories. Whether it was Wanamaker's in Philadelphia, Marshall Field's in Chicago, Hudson's in Detroit, Rich's in Atlanta, Filene's in Boston, or Famous-Barr in St. Louis, many household names have been relegated to retailing history.

If I had lived in Chicago, for example, I would be attached to Marshall Field's. It would remind me of Frango mints, the parade, and taking my children to see Santa Claus. If I had lived in Philadelphia, I would have joined the throngs of people at Wanamaker's every Christmas to see the holiday light show and listen to the pipe organ. Every major city had a special retailer which became part of growing up there. If these had been my experiences, I would feel that today something special has disappeared from retailing. The individual identities of place have slipped away under consolidation. Federated, which combined a dozen nameplates under the Macy's brand, sincerely tries to recreate that atmosphere of familiarity, but so far, I believe there are many unhappy consumers yearning for something more.

We are raising a new generation that is very comfortable shopping on the Internet, utilizing home shopping on TV, and ordering from catalogs, which raises the key question: Will the department store be as important to future generations as it was to previous ones?

As I try to visualize the world twenty years from now, if the mid-market department store is to retain its importance, it needs to reinvent itself considering the impact of the Internet, consolidation, and globalization. How? Retailers need to become more exciting, entertaining; and more multichannel through direct marketing and the Internet and for some, by becoming a global brand. The opportunities and challenges for upscale retailers appear to be somewhat different. There are increasing numbers of affluent consumers interested in quality shopping, be it at a Neiman Marcus, Saks Fifth Avenue, Bloomingdale's, Barneys, or Bergdorf. With an increase in affluent, well-traveled global customers, this segment of retailing is likely to maintain its importance as a multichannel retailer. In addition, in our evolving societies, there are increasing numbers of aspirational consumers who derive satisfaction from luxury retailers and luxury lifestyle brands.

In 1993, I wrote "retailing is all about change." That is still very true today and the eleven concepts I discuss in this section will impact retailing in the coming decades and influence the future importance of midmarket and upscale department stores.

ELEVEN PRINCIPLES FOR THE COMING DECADES OF RETAILING

When I supervised Bloomingdale's, retailing was very simple: The stores were American stores; the brands were American or European. But in the last decade, the growing globalization of business and the increasing affluence of the developing world has changed everything.

The luxury business is new to the Middle East—the United Arab Emirates only became a country thirty-seven years ago. China has become important in the past twenty years, shifting from Mao suits and bicycles to Louis Vuitton and Polo Ralph Lauren. India has 200 million of their 1 billion people who want to buy branded consumer goods. At the same time, very few international retailers have figured out how to make money in India or China. Most of the opportunity for future growth, in my opinion, will come from outside the United States. Consequently, ten years from now the world could be very different.

1. Globalization
2. Consolidation
3. E-Commerce
4. Technology
5. Home Shopping
6. The Retailer of the Future
7. Redefining the Shopping Center
8. The New Luxury
9. The New Consumers
10. Changing Standards for Department Stores
11. Is There a Role for the Great Merchants?

1. GLOBALIZATION

I have long believed in globalization. In terms of retail, the world is one. It used to be that American brands, with few exceptions, had no interest in overseas markets. Now, an ever-increasing number of American wholesale and retail brands feel that their future growth will be in overseas markets.

The main driver of this new interest is the maturing of the American retail market, which results in slower growth. Brands, seeking new ways of growing, are opening their own retail stores or looking to overseas markets. Concurrent with the maturing of the American market is the enormous growth in the Middle East, Moscow, China, India, Brazil, and perhaps Eastern Europe. Over time, people will be looking at other emerging markets in Asia, such as Singapore, Hong Kong, the Philippines, Indonesia, Korea, and even Vietnam. There are opportunities all around the world, and retailers now want to go after them. Who would have expected that Macau would have more gambling revenue than Las Vegas in 2007?

I believe that in the next ten years, the aggressive American retailer or branded manufacturer will be focusing more and more on these markets. Estée Lauder has publicly said it expects to do more than 60 percent of its business outside the United States. Polo Ralph Lauren today is looking for its major growth to come from such international markets as Japan, Europe, the Middle East, Russia, and, in the future, China and India. Calvin Klein, owned by Phillips-Van Heusen, bought back its Italian license to develop the business for itself. The new C.E.O. of Liz Claiborne is looking for international markets to grow his key brands: Juicy Couture, Lucky Brand Jeans, Mexx, and Kate Spade. In 2007, Wal-Mart did $91.4 billion outside of the U.S. L'Oréal reports today that the emerging markets—Asia, Eastern Europe, the Gulf—contribute 33 percent of sales, and the company expects that by 2017 they will contribute 48 percent.

Abercrombie & Fitch has opened a hugely successful estimated $100 million store in London and is planning flagship stores for Japan as well as in Milan and Paris. Even Victoria's Secret, which for years had no intention of expanding overseas, has changed.

Les Wexner has set up an organization to consider an international expansion plan. Major retailers in many overseas markets are eagerly beating a path to the company's headquarters, in Columbus, Ohio. I believe this could double the size of Victoria's Secret in the next decade.

It is clear that the successful retailers and manufacturers of the next century will be those that learn to think globally and take advantage of these new and emerging markets. Interestingly enough, because I believe America produces the best retailers in the world, this will create substantive job opportunities for U.S. retailers willing to travel and work beyond our borders. I would encourage today's business school and college graduates to consider taking jobs abroad.

2. CONSOLIDATION

As mentioned earlier, when I became a retailer, some sixty years ago, department stores were the hallmark and focus of American retail. Profitable department stores sprouted across the United States. I'm not referring only to Federated, Macy's, and Dillard's but also to chains such as Associated Dry Goods, Carson's, Mercantile, Hudson's, and May. There were probably forty major department-store chains fifty years ago. Today, there are ten. The last sixty years has seen the closing and a consolidation of department stores as many famous names—Abraham and Straus, Strawbridge & Clothier, Filene's, Rich's, B. Altman, and Burdines—have been replaced by the Macy's nameplate or have simply shut their doors.

We are down to a very limited number of department stores today. The most dramatic event to happen in our industry, in many years, was Federated's acquisition of May Department Stores in 2005. At that point, Federated had edited down its own nameplates—Macy's, Rich's, Burdines, Lazarus, and The Bon—from seven to two: Macy's and Bloomingdale's. Then it acquired 480 May stores, sold off 80 and renamed the remaining stores Macy's. The theory behind this was to take full advantage of the Macy's Thanksgiving Day parade, the fireworks, the Macy's Flower Show, and Macy's institutional value across the country, creating a national brand. It all makes great good sense. However, thus far, the program is not meeting all expectations.

Macy's has the potential to leverage its volume and has become the exclusive distributor of such brands as Tommy Hilfiger, Martha Stewart, and T. Tahari. Over time, this could become a unique asset, supplying differentiation and margin in all sectors. Terry Lundgren and Sue Kronick are in the process of creating a unique and potentially very powerful retailing organization. While it is clear there have been inevitable bumps in the road, their long-term objective is very clear, and they have consistently moved toward it.

What is the long-term outlook? In my opinion, over time, Macy's customers will embrace the Macy's name and institution. The company will modify and expand its marketing program to win back customers. I believe this strategy makes sense over the long haul. The recent reorganization into four Macy's divisions—with regional "My Macy's" offices to give recognition to local preferences—is a very healthy step forward. It sets a priority of making stores locally relevant.

Simultaneously, the trading up of Bloomingdale's with emphasis on service, higher price points, and greater focus on contemporary and new bridge resources, combined with aggressive expansion, has been healthy and bodes well for continued future growth.

A side benefit for consumers has been the sale of Lord & Taylor. It was once one of the most respected retail names in America, dating back to 1945 when Dorothy Shaver, one of our great merchants, became president of the company. Lord & Taylor was one of the leaders in promoting a generation of talented American sportswear designers including Bonnie Cashin, Tina Leser, and Claire McCardell. However, when Lord & Taylor became part of the May Department Stores, it was homogenized. It lost its uniqueness, its reputation for casual country club and "ladylike" fashion. Now the new owners are giving C.E.O. and president Jane Elfers the chance to bring back the glory days of Lord & Taylor.

Where is consolidation heading in the future? In the United States, there are only a handful of national brands left. There is not much remaining for consolidation. Over time, I believe more and more of the independent stores will be absorbed into regional or national groups, such as Belk, which added Parisian to become a $5 billion regional player.

With fewer stores to sell to, it was inevitable that the consolidation trend would occur on the supply side as well. There are fewer and fewer wholesalers selling to the department stores. And suppliers like Kellwood, Liz Claiborne, and Jones New York are struggling as they have fewer accounts and the stores do more and more of their own product development or work with single-brand suppliers. Some of these well-known names may not be with us in the future, others will focus more on their own retail outlets. For a while, the favorite inside joke in our industry was that one day, there will only be one store left with one supplier, and that store will look at the supplier and say, "I'm sorry, I don't like your line." It's old, but it seems appropriate.

J. C. Penney has in recent years evolved into a new fashion retailer between the mass market and the department store. The addition of Sephora to create a cosmetics department and the development of American Living as a lifestyle brand, cutting across the entire store and created by Global Brand Concepts, a division of Polo Ralph Lauren, could add a new dimension to Penney's. It is, in a sense, the same path that Macy's is taking with Martha Stewart and Tommy Hilfiger, and it should add excitement, something that is needed in today's challenging retail environment. Penney's is taking on a courageous challenge by moving upscale in a difficult retail environment.

Wal-Mart and Target dominate the retail sector. The sales of all the department stores in the United States combined are less than the Target or Wal-Mart volume. Although their strategies differ, both companies are increasing market share. Target, through creative marketing and product development, has created a chic image (some pronounce it Tar-*jay*, French style). Upscale customers feel comfortable shopping in its stores. This is a great platform for future growth.

Another retailer that can combine class with retail growth is Costco, which is built on a unique model that can generate substantial income at very low margins since it is funded largely by membership fees. I believe both Target and Costco can increase their future share of the market and someday will examine the opportunity for overseas expansion as well.

3. E-COMMERCE

Today we live in a world in which each successive generation has grown up with greater familiarity with the Internet. I see it with my own grandchildren. The Internet provides an enormously convenient way to shop. Customers can shop any place, at any time, twenty-four hours a day, seven days a week. The skillful operators of shopping sites have learned to overcome the early disadvantages. They have created virtual models where people can see how they look in a particular garment, zoom and rotate the merchandise, or see the item in various colors before buying. The results: Americans last year spent more online on clothing than they did on computers; 10 percent of all clothing sales are online, totaling more than $22 billion. It is the largest single category online. And each year, e-commerce maintains its position as the fastest growing channel of retail distribution. In 2007, online sales (excluding travel) reached $174.5 billion, accounting for 7 percent of total retail sales. In segments of our business such as books, cameras, computers, and music, the Internet is already the dominant channel for distribution.

As the Internet grows, what more traditional forms of retail will lose market share? It would seem that catalogs are losing market share to the Internet. In some cases, it is deliberate, as some catalogs are encouraging their customers to shop online. It is less costly, quicker, and more efficient.

As e-commerce becomes a more substantial part of retailing, it is likely to become a significant portion of department-store growth. Today, Neiman Marcus Direct is Neiman's top "store." Saks Direct is the number-two store for Saks Fifth Avenue and is on plan to become number one. Macy's Direct is investing heavily for the future and moving toward a $1 billion volume. J. C. Penney does more than $1.5 billion on the Internet. I believe department stores need to become even more innovative within this sector.

4. TECHNOLOGY

E-Commerce is just one aspect of how technology is changing shopping habits. It is all about ease and convenience. Technology will make life easier for the future shopper in a variety of ways. Clearly, Google and other search engines can do the walking for the consumer— locating the place to buy the product and finding the best price. But search engines are also revolutionizing the way retailers spend their advertising dollars. To be listed first on Google is a very good investment, whether you're Neiman Marcus Direct, Macy's Direct, or Target. New Web 2.0 technologies such as Facebook and MySpace are now able to contextualize commerce by connecting like-minded individuals, groups and friends.

New technologies will bring other changes as well. Retailers are now able to track the consumers of their products and learn where all of their products go—thereby discovering how to better spend their marketing dollars. Indeed, almost every aspect of a shopping transaction is going to change. Forecasting sales and markdowns has been the job of the buyers for many generations. Today, technology can do this more rapidly and more effectively, simultaneously replenishing the store's inventory. Even the checkout process can be automated and sped up. Limitations on how much the shopping process can change lie only in the imagination and creativity of those developing the technology.

It is quite likely that the mobile phone, or "m-commerce," can become the ultimate purchasing instrument in the future, offering promotions and pricing opportunities and the ability to order products quickly and efficiently. Cell phones in Japan now have barcode scanners on them to compare prices with the Web.

5. HOME SHOPPING

Television and video shopping, like other forms of shopping, have now been consolidated. Three major channels—QVC, HSN, and ValueVision—remain. It is clear that new approaches will be needed in the future to retain market share and compete with the Internet.

Today, QVC reaches 80 million homes and achieves estimated sales of $5 billion in the U.S. and $6 billion globally. Customers are comfortable with the channel, but there are opportunities to sell a far greater range of products and to more people. I believe that in the future consumers should be able to use their TVs to shop for cars, homes, insurance, and travel. Home shopping in a sense has limited retail space—there are only twenty-four hours in a day, seven days in a week. Home shopping channels must make that time more productive or find additional outside sources of income.

As home shopping evolves, it needs to do more to gain viewers, create more buzz and excitement, add personalities (although some clearly exist), and strengthen its image as an innovative place to shop.

Today, HSN is evolving into a lifestyle branded channel that recognizes promoting brands that it shares with department stores. It's healthy for both the department store and HSN.

Technology will increase the share of market for home shopping. HSN provides customers with on-demand service that can bring up previous programs by classification, so that the customers can order any products they are currently interested in, or review any programs they missed. The technology exists today so that the customer can order simply by pressing a button on the remote control. It does away with the need for a telephone or a computer. This is instant gratification, and in the homes where it exists, it almost doubles the sales.

Like the department store, home shopping can only grow with exciting new merchandise, new brands, and new technology, while increasing sales on its Web site.

6. THE RETAILER OF THE FUTURE

The retailer of the future will be a true multichannel player—one that enhances the traditional department store with an expanded retail presence including a catalog, a Web site, and perhaps the addition of home shopping on television, so that the consumer will be able to shop at his or her favorite store anytime and through a variety of shopping techniques.

The successful retailer of the future will still have to focus on creating an image and excitement across all channels. Technology is simply an asset for doing that. Ultimately, however, it all begins with the product. The big winners in twenty-first century retailing will be those stores that fully take advantage of our ever-changing technology and combine it with great merchandising.

7. REDEFINING THE SHOPPING CENTER

In recent years, shopping centers have seen declining market share and loss of traffic. I believe that the approach to shopping centers will need to be redefined over time. For example, Marvin Traub Associates works with a client in Europe called Value Retail. It runs nine highly focused shopping centers averaging well over $1,000 per square foot, including a hugely successful center called Bicester Village, in a town about one hour by car northwest of London, that achieves more than $1,600 per square foot. Scott Malkin, the C.E.O., developed a new partnership approach. Value Retail subscribes to a unique department-store operating model. There are no tenants and there are no long-term leases. Brands occupy space as licensees, pay a healthy percentage of sales as a royalty, and can be relocated, changed in size, or replaced as in a department store, reflecting a commitment to aggressive merchandising. Value Retail does not consider itself a shopping center company. Its trained merchants work closely with the brands to maximize sales.

Bicester Village has some one hundred and twenty tenants, all on one-year leases. Each pays a percentage of sales, but none pay fixed rent. Scott has an organization of six merchants for each outlet village who work with the tenants to make them successful. The simple formula is that if a store is not successful, Value Retail does not renew the lease. There is a waiting list of people who would like to join the center. This truly creates a partnership between the developer and the retailer. They work together to achieve great productivity. In any given year, about 15 percent of the tenants move, either to larger spaces, smaller spaces, or out altogether.

Although Value Retail operates outlet centers, I have every confidence that the same strategy can work on full price as well—it's a healthy new direction for shopping centers. Considering the decline in traffic and the lack of growth in most centers across the United States, it is timely to introduce a new approach between developer and tenant.

The traditional shopping center consists of one or two anchor department stores, freestanding retail stores, and some sort of food court. I believe the next generation will be much more about lifestyle and creating an atmosphere that is more like an all-inclusive city. This means not just stores but a hotel, offices, apartments, entertainment, movie theaters with a luxury approach, banks, restaurants, automotive dealerships, upscale food stores, and supermarkets.

The relatively new Time Warner Center in New York, which I worked on for four years, typifies this trend, combining the five-star Mandarin Oriental Hotel with an outstanding 65,000-square-foot Whole Foods supermarket, the Shops at Columbus Circle, apartments that sell for as much as $45 million, and Jazz at Lincoln Center. Customers seem happy with all of these elements. In this way, I believe that the shopping center of the future will become much more like a city.

8. THE NEW LUXURY

Luxury retailing used to be thought of as selling very expensive merchandise, such as $20,000 alligator handbags, $50,000 sable coats, or $100,000 watches. The new luxury retailing, however, is everyday luxury—a Starbucks coffee for $4, Tiffany sterling-silver jewelry for $125, or a Coach handbag for $300. Luxury is in the details, like the new movie theater concept, which sells first-class accomodations with wider more comfortable seating, bigger screens, and gourmet snack foods. Today, more and more people with increasing affluence get pleasure from adding luxury to all aspects of their lives. Victoria's Secret has gone from being value-driven to creating a luxury-shopping experience and an aura of fashion associated with its product. My generation can remember the ads, "Calling all men to Barneys," which invited shoppers to buy inexpensive clothing for men and boys. The new Barneys New York typifies the shift from bargain to luxury. Aspirational customers are increasing globally and supporting such brands as Vuitton, the number-one luxury brand in the world.

9. THE NEW CONSUMERS

There are new consumers in the world bringing about major change in retailing. In the United States, young, hip consumers are attracted to the emerging contemporary fashions. A whole new generation of Wall Street businesspeople is driven by a new degree of affluence to shop for luxury brands, buy larger homes, and travel. But the world is changing. Many in the new group of consumers are part of the BRIC nations—Brazil, Russia, India, and China. Some 40 percent of the world's population resides in India and China alone. Both countries have emerging middle classes that in the next ten years will grow larger than the population of the entire United States. Experts believe that by 2050 both China and India will have surpassed the United States in gross national product. With these changes come consumers who have grown up with television, the Internet, and an aspirational desire to own globally recognized brands that confer status on them in their communities. Selling these brands to new consumers is a key objective for global retailers and global brands. But the world's most savvy retailers recognize that it is difficult to make money in China or India today. They are aligning themselves with local partners, so that during the next ten years they can build profitable businesses there.

When I think about the changes that have occurred in these markets, I'm struck by the memory of my first trip to India, thirty years ago. The only car one saw on the street looked like an early Volkswagen. It was called the Ambassador and came in one model and one color—white. Today, India's automobile industry is thriving, and all of the world's global brands compete. The development of the Nano, a $2,500 car by Tata Motors, is an extraordinary step forward, as well as their acquisition of Jaguar and Land Rover, two luxury brands.

As global businesses are put together, there will be a migration of talented personnel. In India, there are a great many expatriates returning to their home country because today they can do better in India than elsewhere. In Dubai, many of the top people come from Australia, South Africa, the United Kingdom, and the United States, as well as the various countries of the Middle East. Many of these emerging markets will be seeking talent, and it will create opportunities for savvy young people who can build very successful, lucrative careers. One wishes that more Americans studied Chinese.

10. CHANGING STANDARDS FOR DEPARTMENT STORES

For the past forty years, I have enjoyed walking through department stores all over the world. Twenty years ago I believed American department stores were far superior in their merchandising, presentation, and creativity to stores in any other place in the world. Ten years ago the gap began to narrow. Today, I believe Harrods in London and Galeries Lafayette in Paris are outstanding and compete favorably with almost any American store. Harrods probably enjoys the finest luxury business of any store in the world, including an extraordinary fine jewelry presentation. Indeed, the levels of excellence have changed dramatically throughout all of Europe. El Corte Inglés in Spain, de Bijenkorf in Amsterdam, La Rinascente in Milan, Le Bon Marché in Paris, and Harvey Nichols and Selfridges in London are dramatically better than they were ten or fifteen years ago.

Stores like Harvey Nichols Dubai, TsUM in Moscow, and Attica in Athens did not exist in their present form ten years ago. This has created major opportunities for upscale and luxury brands to develop their overseas business. There are many more successful stores to sell to. Much of this is spurred by increasingly affluent, brand-driven consumers in all markets. I believe this trend will be heightened during the next decade with a new generation of retailers in the Middle East, China, Russia, Eastern Europe, and Brazil.

11. IS THERE A ROLE FOR THE GREAT MERCHANTS?

I grew up in an era when the great merchants were some of the most respected members of the business community. The roster included Stanley Marcus of Neiman Marcus, Walter Hoving of Tiffany, Adam Gimbel of Saks, Andrew Goodman of Bergdorf Goodman, Jack Straus of Macy's, Sam Walton of Wal-Mart, and overseas, Marcus Sieff of Marks & Spencer and Harry Gordon Selfridge of Selfridges. Today's leadership includes Lee Scott of Wal-Mart; Terry Lundgren of Macy's; Mike Ullman of J. C. Penney; Burt Tansky of the Neiman Marcus Group; Mickey Drexler of J. Crew; Allen Questrom, the former C.E.O. of J. C. Penney, who sits on Wal-Mart's board; and Ralph Lauren, who has vision and creativity and has built a unique global brand. All continue in the tradition of merchandising greatness.

I'm certain there are others I've forgotten. As one looks ahead twenty years, the challenge lies in predicting where the trendsetters, innovators, and creators will come from. I believe that leadership may very well come from those who make the technological breakthroughs necessary to transform retailing. Today's leaders in that sector include Jeffrey Bezos of Amazon, Meg Whitman of eBay, and the young geniuses Sergey Brin and Larry Page, who founded Google. There are always opportunities in retailing. Who finds them and who seizes upon them will be the ongoing challenge and will produce the great merchants of 2040.

Marvin has that rare combination of never-ending challenges and absolute trustworthiness. Our business was never good enough, there was always a new mountain to climb and a new challenge. Yet, at the same time, his word was his bond. When he said something, you knew that you could trust him absolutely. Our greater relationship, however, was on the personal side. We have traveled the world together from a cruise in Turkey, safari in Africa, and the Indonesian Archipelago. That same curiosity and energy which I always saw in business, came out again in his travels. Just visiting the archeological sites in Turkey wasn't enough. He had to make a film of the trip entitled, "Into Africa."

I am certain that there is a secret emergency plan in the city of New York that, if the power ever fails, they'll simply plug Marvin in, and the lights of the city will go on again.

Leonard A. Lauder, The Estee Lauder Companies

AFTERWORD: BLOOMINGDALE'S IN DUBAI

In my sixteen years as a consultant and investment banker, I have never had a project as appealing to me as developing the first international Bloomingdale's. It began in spring 2007 at a luncheon with Terry Lundgren, the chairman, president, and C.E.O. of Macy's and a longtime friend.

"I think it might be time to give consideration to how to expand your business globally," I told him. "Today, Saks Fifth Avenue has licensed partners in Riyadh, Dubai, and Mexico and has announced plans for China and other markets. Harvey Nichols is in Riyadh, Dubai, Hong Kong, Istanbul, and Jakarta and is interested in other markets. Galeries Lafayette has just announced plans to go into Dubai. My client the Al Tayer Group, which I believe is the most professional group in the Middle East, would be very interested in bringing Bloomingdale's to Dubai and the Middle East."

I fully expected Terry to tell me why this proposal did not interest him, as many years ago, Bloomingdale's and Federated walked away from a partnership in Tokyo.

(Above) The Palm Islands—man-made islands in Dubai. I took this photo from a helicopter with Mike Steinberg, former C.E.O. of Macy's West; *(opposite)* Khalid Al Tayer, Terry Lundgren, Obaid Al Tayer, and me in Dubai.

"This could be interesting," Terry said, surprising me. "Let me talk to some of our principals and I will get back to you."

He later called to say, "I'm not ready to make a commitment now, but I am prepared to meet with your team from Dubai to discuss how we could expand."

We held the meeting in New York in April with Terry; Sue Kronick, the vice chair of Macy's; Mike Gould, the chairman and C.E.O. of Bloomingdale's; and from Dubai, Obaid Al Tayer, the chairman and C.E.O. of the Al Tayer Group; Khalid Al Tayer, his nephew in charge of business development; Shireen El-Khatib, the C.E.O. of Al Tayer Insignia, the luxury brand division; and me. In that meeting, our team outlined why Dubai is a wonderful opportunity for Macy's and why our experience in operating the $100 million Harvey Nichols Dubai could be applied to a prospective Bloomingdale's.

In May 2007, Terry Lundgren was the principal speaker at the World Retail Conference in Barcelona. As Terry spoke about future opportunities, he said that his company was "in the early stages of investigating global expansion of the Macy's and Bloomingdale's banners and that a successful international plan held vast potential." Terry added that Macy's was very aware of the overseas expansion of Saks Fifth Avenue, Harvey Nichols, and Galeries Lafayette, and was studying whether that was appropriate for Macy's.

A week after he was back, I called Terry. "Terry, it sounded to me like you were giving out a help-wanted ad."

He laughed. "Marvin, you're right."

Two weeks later, I contacted Terry and told him that the world's greatest mall was being built in Dubai with 12 million square feet of retail space, fourteen hundred stores, six hotels, residences, offices, the world's tallest building, which will feature an Armani Hotel and Residence, as well as the world's largest indoor aquarium. "This is a very exciting project in a very exciting city."

Galeries Lafayette had already taken 190,000 square feet. The mall was scheduled to open in fall 2008–spring 2009, and it would be an ideal place to locate the first international Bloomingdale's, but we had to move quickly. Terry responded that he was interested, and retained Michael Steinberg to represent Macy's. Mike had been at May Department Stores and had worked with me at Bloomingdale's, as executive vice president of home furnishings, then became president of Foley's and the C.E.O. and chairman of Macy's West.

Mike came to Dubai in late June 2007 to meet with us, the people from Dubai Mall, and the other groups that were seeking to bring Bloomingdale's to the Middle East. In Dubai in June, 120 degrees Fahrenheit is a cool day, so we spent most of our time in air-conditioned cars and offices. We had Mike meet our management team and made a presentation, then took him to see the Harvey Nichols store in the Mall of the Emirates—where he could see Dubaians and tourists skiing down a four-thousand foot indoor ski run. Meanwhile, we met with the Emaar company, developer of the Dubai Mall, which did a presentation on why this was to be one of the world's most unique malls. Next, we were invited to make a presentation in New York in August to a review board that Terry had set up. At that point, we were aware of two major competitors. We negotiated for more retail space, and created a 150,000-square-foot apparel, accessories, and cosmetics store, then planned a separate 60,000-square-foot home-furnishings store, similar to the arrangement of the very successful Bloomingdale's branch in Chestnut Hill, Massachusetts. This plan gave us a 210,000-square-foot store, which would be the largest store in the Middle East.

We felt we had an enormous advantage over our competitors. Not only were we the successful operators of nearly one hundred luxury boutiques, including Giorgio Armani, Gucci, Jimmy Choo, Bulgari, Yves Saint Laurent, Bottega Veneta, Loro Piana, and H. Stern, but in our stores, we control most of the major American brands that would be important to Bloomingdale's. In the four years that I served as adviser to the Al Tayer Group, we had arranged to bring in Elie Tahari, Diane von Furstenberg, Juicy Couture, Malandrino, Oscar de la Renta, and a host of successful American brands that would be needed in a Bloomingdale's.

We felt that we would be very good partners with our high degree of professionalism, our strong organization, and our commitment and dedication to the project. In addition, of course, we felt that having the ex-chairman of Bloomingdale's play a role in the project gave us an advantage. However, it was clear that at least one of our competitors was promising to open more stores in more markets and do a bigger business. We were skeptical but remained realistic in our projections. Naturally, we waited with great expectations, and I was delighted when, on September 24, Terry sent me an e-mail.

"Marvin, this is very confidential. We have decided to work with your group. However, your financial proposal is too low." He requested a higher royalty payment.

I was not surprised, and Khalid Al Tayer and I spent the better part of the week drafting a response. We submitted our offer on Friday, September 28. By Monday, it was accepted. The next step would be a "state" visit by Terry Lundgren accompanied by Mike Steinberg, in order that Terry might better understand his new partners and his new overseas market. It was set for the weekend of November 30th. Terry, Mike, and I flew to Dubai on a Friday evening. On Saturday morning, the three of us, along

with Khalid Al Tayer, took a chartered helicopter tour of Dubai. It is an extraordinary sight, with row on row of gleaming new skyscrapers where thirty years ago there was only desert. We flew close to Burj Dubai then out over the water to view a collection of islands newly built from the sea. Subsequently, we toured the Mall of Emirates. Terry enjoyed the indoor ski slope, the upscale stores, and the atmosphere of Dubai as a shoppers' and retailers' paradise. We then visited the Dubai Mall to preview what will soon be the world's largest shopping center including the world's tallest building and largest indoor aquarium. The day ended with a wonderful dinner in a handsome private dining room, the wine cellar at the Park Hyatt. The next day, we toured Kuwait by chartered jet, visited three shopping centers under construction, and returned for a photo shoot. The visit concluded with another fine dinner in the rooftop dining room of the Burj Al Arab, Dubai's most prestigious hotel and restaurant.

Terry and Obaid Al Tayer got to know each other well, and by the end of the visit, it was clear that there was an attitude of mutual trust, respect, and friendship. Terry and Mike were convinced that they had made the correct decision, and we felt good about our new partners.

(From left) The Time Warner Center combines shopping, dining, living, and entertainment. This is the next generation of shopping mall. My new office at 410 Park Avenue with appropriate Bloomingdale's memorabilia—we always refer to the statue as a Bloomingdale's buyer seeking markdown money. Visiting Colette in Paris, where MCM was launched.

During the weekend of February 9th, Mike Gould, the C.E.O. of Bloomingdale's, visited Dubai with Tony Spring, the new president, Jack Hrushka, the senior vice president of store design, and me. On Sunday, we had a breakfast meeting, an exchange of ideas, and made visits to competing malls. We concluded the day at the Mall of the Emirates and our very successful Harvey Nichols store. The Bloomingdale's contingent was properly impressed. On Monday, we took a tour of Dubai, the world's largest construction site: the Burj al Arab hotel, lunch on the seaside terrace of the Ritz, a presentation of Dubai Mall including the world's tallest building, ending with a "hard hat" Mall tour. Mike's enthusiasm grew with each passing hour. By our final private dinner at the Park Hyatt, Obaid, Shireen, Khalid and I felt, as Mike expressed, "this could be the most exciting project Bloomingdale's has ever done."

There were warm feelings, respect, and an enthusiastic desire to collaborate to create something unique. All in all, both visits represented a wonderful beginning. I believe this will be the most satisfying consulting project I have ever undertaken. I am proud to be part of bringing a 210,000-square-foot Bloomingdale's store to one of the world's most exciting malls and cities. My world has come full circle.

A PERSONAL NOTE

Not everyone has two bites at the apple. This book gave me a chance to rethink the fifteen years that have passed since I wrote *Like No Other Store*. I continue to feel that I have been truly blessed with my great and satisfying career. At the same time, I continue to be supported by a wonderful and close family.

My wife, Lee, is a loving and supportive companion and has been a sounding board for me throughout the nearly sixty years of our marriage. Our three wonderful children include Andrew, our bright and very capable eldest son who worked with me in India and in my consulting business until he joined a consulting firm working with clients in the Middle East. Andrew is married to Lois, a dedicated labor lawyer and litigator. Jimmy is our brilliant, globe-trotting journalist who writes thoughtful political and social articles for the *New York Times Magazine* and as of this writing is publishing his sixth book on the changing promotion of democracy worldwide. Jimmy is married to Buffy Easton, who is creating a new, widely praised and much-needed curriculum to train museum curators for museum directorship. Peggy, our outstanding daughter, is a member of the Committee of 200 and has taken a leadership role in women's business organizations. She shares my passion for business and has established an extraordinarily successful global home-furnishings company, Adesso. Her life companion, Phyllis, is a hard-working, dedicated psychiatric social worker.

Our four grandchildren bring much joy. Rebecca is working at a firm supporting hedge funds and is preparing to go to law school after having graduated from Washington University in St. Louis. Rachel, an outgoing and fun-loving sophomore at Washington University, will be working this summer for a movie producer in Hollywood, after having interned at Diane von Furstenberg last summer. Abigail, our youngest granddaughter, has an unusual and inquisitive mind. She recently returned from living with a family in New Zealand and is an aspiring actress and world traveler. Alexander, our grandson, takes after his parents in being articulate, informed, and sophisticated. He spent a very fulfilling half of his junior year away from Collegiate at a farm school in New Hampshire—an outgrowth of Milton Academy. We are fortunate that all of our children and grandchildren live nearby and are able to share our enthusiasm for travel. Now, instead of taking them skiing, we take them on a safari in Kenya or to India for vacation.

We have an extended family as well. In 1965, we adopted a child in Hong Kong through foster parents. Thomas Wei Ching Cheung was then fourteen years old and living with his family in a single room above a tenement. We watched with pride as, years later, he married, came to New York to study marine insurance, returned to Hong Kong, and developed a career first with a local company and then with AIG. In October, he called with great news: "Dad, I've been recruited to become C.E.O. of a publicly traded $100 million cap company." In December, Lee and I had the pleasure of having lunch with Thomas and the founder of his new company.

In 1970, we befriended our Japanese guide Akiko Kawano to the Expo '70 World's Fair, in Osaka, who came to the United States, married an American, and raised two wonderful children—our first "grandchildren." Today, Nathaniel Jones is developing a derivatives business in Europe for JPMorgan Chase, and Natalie Jones is a dedicated attorney at a boutique law firm in Chicago. They are part of our family.

If a consultant is to remain competitive in our rapidly changing retailing environment, it is essential to stay on top of changes in our industry and with our consumers. I keep up in two ways—by being in the stores and by communicating. I enjoy walking through stores and shopping centers, both in the United States and abroad. A good merchant can see very quickly who is doing well and who is not without ever looking at actual numbers.

It is my style to regularly schedule breakfasts or lunches with people I can learn from and discuss what I believe is happening in the retailing world, so that it can be a two-way conversation. Typically, I breakfast at the Regency and lunch at the Four Seasons, so the food and surroundings are good as well. I want to publicly thank those good friends and fellow diners who keep me in the loop: Burt Tansky of the Neiman Marcus

(Following pages) The Traubs on safari in Kenya, 2004.

Group; Terry Lundgren and Sue Kronick of Macy's; Mike Gould of Bloomingdale's; James Gold of Bergdorf Goodman; Ron Frasch and Stephen Sadove of Saks Fifth Avenue; Howard Socol of Barneys; Roger Farah, Jeff Sherman, and Jeff Morgan of Polo Ralph Lauren; Arnold Aronson of Kurt Salmon Associates; Leonard and William Lauder of Estée Lauder; Jane Elfers of Lord & Taylor, Lester Gribetz, Frank Doroff of Bloomingdale's; Arnold Cohen of Mahoney Cohen; and Larry Leeds of Buckingham Capital Management.

GIVING BACK

I have always considered myself very fortunate to have multiple careers; a great marriage with a loving partner; happy, successful children; grandchildren to whom we are close; and good health for both Lee and me—despite the wounds I incurred in World War II.

Clearly, I am blessed, and I believe in giving back to the community. Earlier in my career, I served on the development committees of the Metropolitan Museum of Art and Lincoln Center, and the boards of the Fashion Institute of Technology, the Hospital for Joint Diseases, the Phoenix Theater, and the Asia Society, among others.

However, my greatest extracurricular interest has always been in education. In 1985, we created the Lee and Marvin Traub Scholarship Program at Harvard College. Its only criteria are that students come from middle-income families and be in the top half of their class. Harvard selects the students, and we typically help them in their sophomore year and beyond. Usually we have five students each year, since inception we have supported almost fifty scholars. We travel to Cambridge every April to take our scholars to dinner and to learn about them. In turn, they learn about us. We consider them to be part of our extended family. We have met some wonderful youngsters through the program. We've attended their weddings, met their children—and of course helped in their careers. We helped to place one aspiring theater executive as an assistant to the producer for the Broadway hit *Spring Awakening,* we met with the judge whom another recipient clerked for, and placed others with Burdines and Saks. We have held two reunions for these scholars, and it is very satisfying to watch their careers.

Currently, I serve on the board of Parsons The New School for Design. I have been active at Harvard College, Harvard Business School, the Harvard School of Public Health, and I cochaired our twenty-fifth to forty-fifth Harvard Business School reunions, then chaired the fiftieth. And I've just joined the advisory council to the dean of the John F. Kennedy School of Government. I serve as adviser to an Indian student there. Lee and I were pleased that I could share this activity with our daughter, Peggy, who funds an intern program at the Kennedy School and is on the women's advisory board.

I have also discovered that I enjoy teaching, and have taught classes at Brown, the Wharton School of the University of Pennsylvania, Brandeis, Harvard Business School, and at the Columbia Business School, where I now conduct one class every semester in the retailing curriculum. In addition to my work in education, I still make it a priority to continue my activities on behalf of the Asia Society and the United Nations.

Lee, of course, is very dedicated to dance. I believe she has made a great contribution as chairperson and supporter of the Martha Graham Center, and later as a board member of Pascal Rioult Dance Theatre. She's been involved in a host of other activities in the dance world, and marked eleven years of service on the board of the New 42nd Street, the nonprofit that has revitalized Forty-second Street. She has been an active volunteer all her life including working with HIV/AIDS patients and in the administration of former mayor Ed Koch.

GIVING THANKS

A special heartfelt thanks and appreciation to Sue Kronick. She is not only an extraordinary, talented merchant, but a great leader. I am very proud—she wrote the foreward for this book. I also want to take this opportunity to thank Lisa Marsh, a *Women's Wear Daily*–trained journalist, who has been a great partner in putting together

Like No Other Career. She has given up many weekends so we could collaborate. Lee and I have learned to love her daughter, Lillian, who swam in our pool while Lisa and I worked together. And then her son, Daniel, joined us. He was born into the world as we were giving birth to this book. It has been fun working with Lisa.

And to Amy Hafkin and Natalie Bozoyan, my great appreciation for their diligent efforts and very long hours. A thanks to Nigel French and Walter Loeb for their considerable assistance. And a thanks to Erika Imberti for her patience with the author and his corrections.

A great appreciation to Morty Singer for his invaluable advice and help in making me knowledgeable and relevant in e-commerce, technology, and current trends.

And very special thanks to Lee Traub, for keeping my grammar and punctuation honest and serving as an invaluable sounding board for *Like No Other Career*. You're a terrific partner.

When I was approached by Assouline's editorial director, Esther Kremer, about this project, I knew that collaborating with Marvin Traub would be the chance of a lifetime. I'd like to thank her for the opportunity.

Working with Marvin on this book has been an incredible journey, one that I will never forget. Through his eyes and experiences, I feel as though I've traveled along for the dealmaking in Dubai, Mumbai, Moscow, Iceland, and New York—all while working from his study in Greenwich, Connecticut. I thank his wonderful wife, Lee, for her hospitality, particularly when it came to showing my precocious and inquisitive two-year-old what seemed like every nook and cranny in her house.

Also indispensable to me are Ben Winters and his colleagues: Team Lillian—Laura Mangan, Mabusi Mbili, Maura Figueroa, and Yanelis "Jenny" Navarro; Team Daniel— Ginger Mangan, Joanne Marsh, Lesly de Groot Axelrod, and Kathleen Ferrall; the incredible poker-playing and playgroup moms of Hudson Heights; and finally, Dan Mangan, the best partner a woman could have and a devoted father to Lillian Mabel and Daniel Joseph, our most important projects.

—Lisa Marsh

MARVIN TRAUB'S PROJECTS: A TIMELINE

November 1991 I leave Bloomingdale's and move to the Federated Department Stores.

February 1992 I leave Federated and create Marvin Traub Associates with Lester Gribetz in Carnegie Hall Towers. Clients include Polo Ralph Lauren, Jones New York, American Express, and Federated Department Stores.

1993 QVC with Diane von Furstenberg and Barry Diller | Saks Fifth Avenue—Japan | Lane Crawford/Balbina Wong—China

1994 Block Industries—Big & Tall—Andrew Traub, C.E.O. | Prime Retail—named to the board of directors. | Conran's Habitat—with Lester Gribetz, Carl Levine, Helaine Suval, and Peggy Traub | Founded Iman Cosmetics with Lester Gribetz and Joe Spellman | association with Financo

1995 Johnnie Walker Collection—Jim Furyk | *Men's Health* magazine | Quartier 206 Berlin—August Jagdfeld | Elizabeth Taylor—Avon

1996 Yue-Sai Kan—We help her sell the company, twice. | Gruppo Coin—major Italian retailer | Adesso—Peggy Traub

1997 Shanghai Tang—David Tang | Sweet16.com—e-commerce—Britney Spears

1998 Pout Cosmetics | Lanvin—L'Oréal

1999 Chairman of Nautica Europe | Licensing Isaac Mizrahi—Lucy Perada—Target (Earth Works)

2000 First trip to Middle East—Kuwait—Al-Shaya Group | Mercury Group—Moscow—TsUM—Alla Verber

2001 Create Financo Global Consulting | Provell board | Beirut project—Tony Salame—Aishti | Home Company | India Conference, Delhi

2002 Time Warner Center | Start with Al Tayer Group in Dubai—Harvey Nichols Dubai | Mortimer Singer joins Marvin Traub Associates | Holt Renfrew—Andrew Jennings—Canada

2003 The Museum Company chairman | Wangfujing Department Stores—China | Carpet One—Liz Claiborne license | Innovative Marble and Tile—funding/consulting | Oscar de la Renta—retail expansion | Linens 'n Things—new store concepts

2004 China—Miles Kwok—Phyllis George | Scott Barnes Cosmetics | Trump Ocean Club International Hotel and Tower—Panama | Kishore Biyani—India | See that Again/Star Styles Internet | Grant Boxing | Oscar de la Renta—retail strategy | Alessandro Dell'Aqua—Claude Arpels | Kelly Hoppen

2005 Sell Stuart Weitzman | Indian Fashions—Lord & Taylor | Move to 350 Park Avenue, leave Financo | Senior adviser to Compass Advisers—Stephen Waters | Sell Slatkin Candles to The Limited—with Compass Advisers | Harvey Nichols Dubai launch | Le Silla shoes | Lenny Kravitz | Drinks Americas board | chairman—SD Retail Consulting—Shopper's Stop—India | Lane Crawford—Hong Kong/Shanghai | Elie Tahari | Eren Group— Istanbul | Attica Group—Athens | Perry Advisers

2006 Move to 825 Third Avenue | Trump Vodka | The Plaza—Elad Properties | LL Cool J | Tata Industries—India | Trent retail—India | MCM—Sung-Joo Kim | TowerBrook Capital Partners (acquires Jimmy Choo) Chairman—SD Retail Consulting | Té Casan shoes board | Deerfoot Meadows, Calgary, Canada

2007 Kira Plastinina—Moscow | Join board of NexCen | Polo Ralph Lauren launch—Moscow | Move to 410 Park Avenue | Create TSM Capital | Matthew Williamson | Bloomingdale's Dubai

2008 André Benjamin | Ellen Tracy

THE BLOOMINGDALE'S ALUMNI CLUB

Fifteen years ago, in *Like No Other Store*, I listed twenty-nine Bloomingdale's executives who, after working with me, became principals of significant entities. Since then, ten more have joined the group, and seven of the initial twenty-nine have moved on to newer and larger responsibilities.

NEW PRINCIPALS (SINCE 1993):

Paula Bennet | *president, J. Jill*

Susan Davidson | *group president, Liz Claiborne; president of NRDC Equity Partners*

John Demsey | *president, Estée Lauder Company*

James Gold | *president and C.E.O., Bergdorf Goodman*

Barbara Kennedy | *president, Ralph Lauren Dresses*

Ronald Klein | *chairman and C.E.O., Macy's East*

Joann Langer | *president, Alvin Valley*

Paul Raffin | *C.E.O., Frette*

Glen Senk | *C.E.O., Urban Outfitters; president, Anthropologie*

Matthew Serra | *chairman and C.E.O., Foot Locker*

ADDED OR CHANGED RESPONSIBILITIES:

Robin Burns | *C.E.O., Victoria's Secret Beauty*

Gordon Cooke | *C.E.O., J. Jill*

Mickey Drexler | *chairman and C.E.O., J. Crew*

Susan Kronick | *vice chair, Macy's, Inc.*

Denise Seegal | *C.E.O. and president, Nautica Enterprises*

Jeff Sherman | *C.E.O., The Limited Stores; president and C.O.O., Ralph Lauren*

Mark Shulman | *president, Filene's Basement*

In the 25 years that I have known Marvin, he has been the unrelenting optimist, always looking for and generally finding the next great opportunity. He is as well-connected today, years after his "retirement" from Bloomingdale's, as he was as its chairman. This gives his insights special standing because they are so well-founded in historical perspective, only updated and contemporized. In our many discussions, he has always affirmed for me the wisdom of keeping my mind active and my feet moving, especially as it concerns markets outside the United States. Marvin was an internationalist before having a global strategy became de rigueur. The way Marvin has managed his career, his affairs and his life is exemplary, and a road map for those of us fortunate to have been blessed by his touch.

Paul Charron, former C.E.O. of Liz Claiborne, Inc.

All photographs and artworks are courtesy of Marvin Traub, with the exception of the following: p. 8, 80: Courtesy of Home Furnishings News, © Corbis; Nick Machalaba/*WWD* © Condé Nast Publications; p. 11: © Jean-Michel Berts; p. 16-17: © Jose Fuste Raga/Corbis; p. 19, 21:Courtesy of Diane von Furstenberg; p. 25: MGM/The Kobal Collection; p. 67: Courtesy of Lanvin; p. 71: George Chinsee/*WWD* © Condé Nast Publications; p. 77-73: Courtesy of Shanghai Tang; p. 80: © Clint Spaulding/PatrickMcMullan.com, Calabrese & Eichner / *WWD* © Condé Nast Publications, David Turner/ *WWD* © Condé Nast Publications, p. 89: Dimitrios Kambouris/WireImage ; p. 91: Courtesy of the *Calgary Herald*; p. 94: © Joe Schildhorn/PatrickMcMullan.com; p. 96: © Daniel Karmann/dpa/Corbis; p. 104-105: © Luca Da Ros/ Grand Tour/Corbis; p. 116-117: © Tibor Bognar/Corbis; p. 119: Cheol H. Park by MCM USA; p. 125: Design: Arias Serna Saravia S.A.—Bogotá, Colombia, Render: Oruga—Bogotá, Colombia.; p. 132: © Allesandra Benedetti/Corbis; p. 134: *WWD*/© Condé Nast Publications; p. 137: Courtesy of *New York* magazine; p. 141: Courtesy of *WWD*/© Condé Nast Publications.

The publisher wishes to thank the following people for their help and contributions to this book: Corinne Tapia of Sous Les Etoiles; Dilcia Johnson from Corbis; Emese Szenasy of Diane von Furstenberg Studio, L.P.; Jean-Michel Berts; Jennifer Algoo at Patrick McMullan; Larry Van Cassele from Getty Images; Lisa Marsh; Luc Alexis Chasleries; Michael Gambardella of McFadden Publishing Inc.; Monica Zurowski of the *Calgary Herald*; Nancy Shore; Natalie Bozoyan and Amy Hafkin of Marvin Traub Associates; Nell Chen at MCM New York; Ricky Byrd from The Kobal Collection; Rodrigo Rubio Vollert of EVP Architecture and Design; Serena Torrey of New York Media; and Tricia Gesner and Alexandra Bernet from Condé Nast Publications.

Every possible effort has been made to identify legal claimants; any errors and omissions brought to the publisher's attention will be corrected in subsequent editions.

MERCI A CE GRAND HOMME,

AMÉRICAIN DU NORD,

RUSÉ ET GENTILHOMME,

VALEUREUX DANS L'EFFORT.

INGENIEUSEMENT,

NEW-YORK A ÉPOUSÉ

TRAUB, QUI PAR SON TALENT

RÉANIMA, QUEL EXPLOIT!,

AVEC PASSION ET FOI,

URBI, ORBI, A MA GRANDE JOIE

BLOOMINGDALE'S, LE ROI...

des
magasins de
New-York!

Jean-Louis Dumas, C.E.O. of Hermès, began his retailing career as a Bloomingdale's trainee. Equipped with great taste and flair, he made Hermès a widely respected billion-dollar global brand. He loved to sketch and always traveled with a small spiral notebook. I suspect this unique sketch came from that book. I am appreciative that he supplied the folio for the artwork as well.